SWEATING FROM YOUR EYES

EMOTIONAL FITNESS FOR MEN

SWEATING FROM YOUR EYES

EMOTIONAL FITNESS FOR MEN

BY
DAVE LONEY

A GROWORKS COACHING BOOK

Cover design by Tim Urquart of Bang On! Design (www.bangon.ca)

Printed in Canada.

Library and Archives Canada Cataloguing in Publication

Loney, Dave 1960-
Sweating From Your Eyes: Emotional Fitness for Men/by Dave Loney

ISBN 0-9733586-4-5
1. Self-actualization (Psychology) 2. Men--Psychology. I. Title
BF561.L65 2004   158.1'081   C2004-904538-5

Published in partnership with
Fresh Wind Press
5647-248th Street
Aldergrove, BC, Canada V4W 1C4
www.freshwindpress.com

CONTENTS

The Emotional Zones

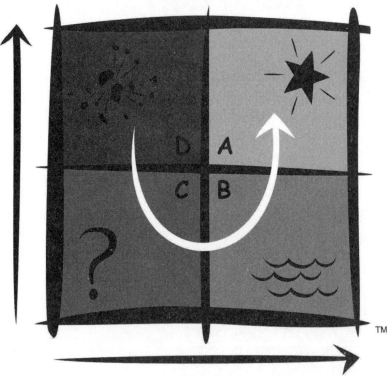

ENDORSEMENT

In recent years, much has been written concerning the problems men face in our society. These messages are designed to counteract a lifestyle that stresses doing over being, skill over character, production over enjoyment, and materialism over spirituality. A man lacking in character, spirituality, and the ability to be true to himself seeks his identity through jobs and material possessions instead.

Trained mental health professionals have written a variety of books that address these problems. Similarly, leadership and management consultants have lent their expertise. Religious professionals from various faith persuasions have also pointed toward what matters most.

However, one of the most powerful mediums for effective communication is the willingness of one person to open up his or her life. I believe this is where some of the experts may struggle. Mental health workers can maintain professionalism by hiding behind concepts and theories. Consultants may keep their personal lives hidden from view as they offer perspectives on leadership and management. Clergy can hide from the truth they seek to impart by failing to describe or demonstrate how it has worked in their own lives. When this happens, competence and credibility are hard to assess, authenticity is difficult to measure, and genuine integrity is obscured from view. Why? Because the personal story is missing.

Herein lies the strength of this book. In *Sweating from Your Eyes*, Dave offers practical concepts, discusses important principles, and talks about spirituality. But most importantly, he uses his own life as the primary illustration. He does not present himself as a perfect traveler driving in a nicely polished car, well tuned, and filled with gas. Rather, he is a fellow pilgrim with struggles in his family of origin, marriage, parenting, and life. He shares his failures and successes willingly without a condescending or prideful attitude. And when he does, it always brings hope and healing.

As you are invited to think more deeply about your own life, it is my hope that Dave's story will help you put doing, skill, production and materialism in their rightful place—behind being, character, enjoyment, and spirituality. Then the truth Dave speaks about will really set you free.

Dr. Rod Wilson
President/Professor of Counseling and Psychology
Regent College
Vancouver, BC

FOREWORD

I know firsthand that outward success can cover feelings of fear and failure. The notoriety I have experienced in my life has served to mask my inner sense of loneliness and despair. However, I have also learned that true peace and contentment come from understanding myself from the inside and becoming emotionally fit.

Dave Loney has learned this as well. In *Sweating From Your Eyes*, Dave has put into words the principles that have worked so well in my own life. For instance, he has grasped a truth that I can validate—in order to change, I had to shed my strong-guy image and take an honest look at myself. I needed input from others, time to reflect and pay attention to the state of my soul.

Dave has "field tested" these principles in real life—in his own life, in the founding and operating of a successful corporation, in the facilitating and guiding men's growth groups, and in one-on-one coaching and mentoring relationships. They apply to men from all walks of life, and, if followed, they can become life changing.

Throughout *Sweating from Your Eyes*, Dave's physical fitness metaphors illustrate the training needed to achieve emotional fitness. I quickly grasped his use of the Zones that describe the emotional state in which men tend to live and how they apply to my life. Am I living in the *Actualizing Zone*, strong both on the outside and inside and building a firm lasting legacy? Do I dwell in the *Destructive Zone*, where I appear outwardly strong but my inner weaknesses and anger create havoc in my life and the lives of others? Do I get trapped in the *Can't Zone?* Or am I able to reflect positively and build strength of character in the *Being Zone?*

Dave's book is written in an easy-to-read style, and men will relate to his experiences and vulnerability. This frees them to share hurts, fears, and anger that block their personal happiness, growth, and success. His struggle with the effects of physical abuse have forced him to discover and overcome his anger and fear of rejection in order to become the well-balanced leader, husband, father, and friend that he is today. Because Dave has overcome his own struggles, he knows that others can as well.

This book can start a chain reaction in your life that will fill you with a sense of well being that you never thought possible. Although reading it is important, the real benefits come from practicing Dave's emotional exercises on a daily basis. They are based on timeless principles that work. He provides some excellent suggestions to gain emotional strength, such as finding workout buddies or a coach to help you obtain your emotional fitness goals. If you choose this route, it can be an exciting, exhilarating journey, one that lasts a lifetime. Once you start, you will never want to go back.

Bon Voyage!

Paul Henderson
Founder and President of The Leadership Group
Former Team Canada Member

PREFACE

Early in 2000, I made a difficult decision to leave the corporate training business I had co-founded twelve years earlier. The company, Eagle's Flight®, had sprung to life in a Toronto basement and grown rapidly from there. We began by marketing a training game called *Gold of the Desert Kings*™. It simulates the incredible pressure we all face to get moving, to show progress in the face of competition and peer pressure. You could not win the game though, without taking time to assess all of the pertinent information—a powerful lesson on the value of planning.

At age 27, I began to market the company's products and services. But who would listen to me, another well-dressed man with something to offer major companies dealing with huge management and change issues? I needed a hook, an "in," so that I could create a first impression that matched our unique experiential training products. I decided the suit had to go. I went into boardrooms wearing a pith helmet and khakis. The image worked. Within three years, sales were over a million dollars.

While building the company, we relied on gut-level instincts to make the right decisions at the right time. We took product design and marketing risks, and I loved that. When I left, Eagle's Flight was approaching the $10 million-a-year sales mark and had employees and associates around the world. But my passion lay in beginning new ventures. It was time to go.

Walking away from my partners' camaraderie was difficult. I also faced breaking off regular contact with other relationships I had formed along the way. For example, when Eagle's Flight was four or five years old, we joined the *Instruction Systems Association,* which brings together forward-thinking organizations involved in the training and development industry. Members gather on a regular basis, including an annual summit meeting in Arizona. As a board member, I worked with other elected officials to help the organization meet its mandate and developed some deep friendships. After deciding to leave Eagle's Flight, I attended one last association meeting to say good-bye.

We met at a five-star Arizona hotel. Wandering down immaculately manicured paths, past flowering cacti, landscaped gardens, and swimming pools, I realized this place had become a home away from home for me. My family visited often, and fond memories filled my mind. Both my professional colleagues and the surroundings inspired me.

I began to question my rationale for leaving. After saying my last good-byes and exchanging hugs and handshakes, I meandered back to my hotel room to pack, overwhelmed with a sense of loss and self-doubt. Later, while picking up some presentation materials in an empty conference room, a member of the association's administrative team approached me.

"Dave, have you been crying?" She asked.

I laughed. "No, I've been sweating from my eyes."

"Wow, that's a cool way of saying it."

I made a mental note of her reaction to my "less than macho" admission. Then went home to contemplate my future.

TIME FOR REFLECTION

My wife Cathy and I live on a beautiful piece of land. Mature cedar trees line the property's north side. A 100-year-old pine and spruce forest nestles behind the cedars, and then merges into a mature maple and beech woodland. A birch, poplar, and cedar-forested wetland stretches beyond these timberlands. Each area has a distinct smell, look, and texture. You can wander over a three-quarter-mile stretch and experience four different ecosystems.

Several years ago, we fenced off a pasture between the woodlands, incorporating some of the forest to make a natural habitat for elk. We decided to breed elk for economic reasons as well as for the beauty these majestic creatures added to the property. They also represented a symbolic statement: I had chosen to stay home. No more meetings, business deals or flights to the seventeen countries in which Eagle's Flight had established businesses over the past ten years. The elk helped me to settle down, pause, and examine my life. I had always been a risk-taker, but I had chosen to wait before determining my next steps.

As I worked with the elk, heaving bales of straw and mending fences, I reflected on this new stage of my life. I determined to let go of the past and make plans that would build on my strengths and core principles. At times, emotions overwhelmed me and my eyes welled with tears. Quietly, I would start *sweating from my eyes* for no apparent reason. My lifestyle change allowed pent-up anxiety and inner turmoil to surface. The tears purged many toxic emotions.

Taking time to pause and reflect proved productive. In addition to helping me work through my own emotional issues, it also gave me new direction in life, a chance to uncover the principles of emotional fitness that I share in this book. Along with writing this book, I have also established *Groworks Coaching, Inc.,* an organization dedicated to enabling executives and entrepreneurs to attain both personal and professional life balance through self-discovery, personal alignment, innovative instruction and coaching. I trust you will also enjoy the benefits that came from this time of reflection and growth.

Dave Loney

INTRODUCTION

Face it: As men, we are far more willing to work on our physical fitness than prepare for life's emotional trials. Physical workouts help us maintain control. We admire guys with great physiques and believe they can handle any situation. Physical strength rules.

However, our unwillingness to deal with our feelings has cost us—big time. Our marriages are falling apart. We cannot communicate with our kids. And our lack of friendships leaves us feeling puny, angry, isolated, and helpless. So we set up walls. We compartmentalize our lives. We ignore conflicts, hoping they will go away. But they do not. And when we are forced to face them, we do not know what to do.

As our emotional pain builds, we try to medicate it with drugs, sex or alcohol. If a loved one gives us an ultimatum—Change or else!—we turn to the myriad of resource materials that proclaim the need for character, integrity, and communication. But while many of them offer encouraging platitudes, they do not show us how to develop habits that build such emotional well being.

Having been down this road too many times myself, I have written this book to address the emotional side of our lives that we have long ignored. I am not a psychologist, but I have studied, discussed, and applied the truths and principles in this book for many years. *Sweating From Your Eyes: Emotional Fitness for Men* contains simple exercises that, if practiced, can help you become the

Rolling with life's punches will not give us enough exercise or endurance to win the emotional game.

man you want to be—one who is in control of his life with the inner strength to lead his family, co-workers, and community.

Just as an athlete trains to stay in top shape, we need to do the same on an emotional and spiritual level. Rolling with life's punches will not give us enough exercise or endurance to win the emotional game. We have to actively pursue an emotional fitness program.

We would be foolish to try and dead lift 300 pounds the first time we went to the gym. Yet we attempt to lift gigantic emotional burdens—like a parent's death, a wife's breast cancer or a runaway teenager—all the time without having our emotional feet planted properly. We slog through grueling emotional marriage and parenting marathons without proper training and end up hurting others and ourselves as a result.

If you have been dragging around emotional "fat" all these years, I want to show you how to lose it. If you are too "lean" and have underdeveloped or locked emotional muscles, I want to help you release that stiffness, strengthen your character, and overcome bad habits.

This book will help you gain the strength, balance, and co-ordination needed to achieve positive results. It will also help you build and maintain quality relationships. By making changes in your lifestyle and disciplining your mind, you can become a powerhouse of emotional strength.

EMOTIONS AND HEALTH

The connection between physical and emotional health is common knowledge. Perhaps you have read about the driven, angry person who is prone to heart attacks. You may also know about the correlation between anxiety and diseases like cancer. People with positive outlooks tend to contract fewer illnesses and recover faster when they do fall sick.

We all live in stressful environments. Some of us react in anger, creating additional stress for those around us. Others bottle up or block out their emotions, weakening their immune systems.

Maybe you are one of these men. You know you are an emotional wreck—or on the way to becoming one. How would you like to resolve your inner conflicts before your skyrocketing blood pressure forces you into the hospital? You can learn how to respond to stress in ways that make you stronger, not weaker.

Emotionally fit men are at peace with themselves and those around them. Their happiness is genuine. They do not hide behind plastic smiles, false bravado or macho images. Well-balanced men handle conflicts without backing down or lashing out. Strong yet even-tempered, they live a life of integrity and truthfulness. Their wives and children love and respect them. When leadership is needed at home, the workplace or the community, these men can be depended upon. They are not pushovers; they are real men. And you can become one of them.

> *Emotionally fit men are at peace with themselves and those around them. Their happiness is genuine.*

MAD AT THE WORLD

No matter your background or the shape you are in, you can change your character and emotional and spiritual make-up. I speak from experience. A childhood full of physical abuse left me mad at the world, deeply insecure and self-destructive.

My father was a doctor, and we were reasonably well off financially. However, Dad's unpredictable and often brutal punishment drove me into a vicious cycle of resentment, rebellion, and further abuse. I hated him. By the time I hit grade nine, my heartache and self-destructive behavior were leading me straight to jail—or worse.

That summer, a terrible accident and an excruciating three-month hospital stay in the burn unit forced me to think about my actions and consequences. A friend and I took some latex gloves and a propane torch to a nearby park, filled the gloves with propane, and pinned them to a picnic table. Then we threw matches at them, awestruck by the roaring bursts of flame.

Around that time, I had also found an oxygen stick made of sulfurous material. It was in my pocket. While throwing matches, the oxygen stick caught fire; burning a hole in my thigh and releasing concentrated oxygen around me. In a panic, I slapped my thigh, thinking the pain was from bee stings. Then my hand started to burn in front of my eyes, and I dove to the ground, rolling in agony. Fortunately, the stick fell away from my body. Terrified, I ran home and jumped into the bathtub, turning the shower on full cold. Then my mother wrapped me in a towel and rushed me to the emergency ward.

While I went through painful treatments, my family moved households within Toronto. I considered this as a chance to start my life over. I wanted a radical change. Instead of being a loner at school, I wanted success, popularity, and good grades. Though not especially good at team sports, I knew that being athletic lead to popularity, so I started working out to build my physique, my self-esteem, and to gain the approval of others.

ACTING CLASS

Learning how to get along with people and influence their perceptions of me was not easy. So, in grade ten, I enrolled in a theatre arts program to hone my image. I believed that acting more confidently and assertively would help me achieve my goals.

My teacher and classmates taught me how to change the way I came across to others. I learned to control my thoughts and fears, settle my mind, and listen to others and myself. Roles in various school plays helped me discover how to empathize with different characters. I focused on becoming a different person on the outside but never let anyone know how I felt inside.

By the end of grade eleven, I had attained my goals, and success followed me everywhere. But these outer changes did not make me happy. My physique, clothes, speech, and smile were a disguise. A smokescreen. I came home after wild parties bawling my eyes out, feeling desperate and lost, the real me hidden behind a façade. My inner pain ravaged me, and I could not escape the emptiness I felt.

My shallow character led to bad choices, and I wrestled constantly against destructive anger and lashing out at others. I looked strong, but inner weakness prevailed. I feared others would discover my fraudulent self, and so I cycled between victim and victimizer, looking to relationships, sex, and friends—anything to help me out. But my actions only took me further away from what I really needed—character and emotional health.

> *I focused on becoming a different person on the outside but never let anyone know how I felt inside.*

Perhaps you can identify with my struggle. Maybe you had a physically and verbally abusive father, too. Or maybe he was emotionally absent and spent his days sitting in front of the TV while your mom played drill sergeant. We have all been wounded in some way. Rarely have I met a man who does not suffer from some kind of "father hunger."

A CHANGED LIFE

When dating my wife, Cathy, I hid my emptiness carefully. She came from a sheltered, stable home and had no idea of the turmoil and anger lurking inside me. When the truth started to leak out, it was extremely painful for both of us. Thank God she was willing to work through the hard times with me.

When Cathy became pregnant, I dreaded the prospect of fatherhood and feared inflicting my damaged emotions on our children. When my boys were small, I would get upset or impatient over little things. Though never physically abusive, my irritability and anger hurt Cathy and our children. My sons retreated from me. Fear of me gripped them whenever they made mistakes, and they sought out their mom instead of me when they needed something. I did not want Cathy to play the same role as my mother did, cushioning her children against her husband's anger and excusing my bad moods to my children. Desperate to be a loving husband and father, I began with the steps outlined in this book.

Cathy and I have been married for over twenty years now, and we are deeply in love. She is my best friend. We share a tender, affectionate relationship, but our growth has not come easily. Our three children are nearing adulthood, and yet my two strapping sons, Alex and Benji, often embrace me after a day at school. They share their deepest secrets, personal struggles, and victories with me. We also have a lovely and confident daughter, Natalie, who we trust to make wise choices in life. She and I share a special bond, too. My family's success means more to me than my success as an entrepreneur and leader. But I have learned I can have both.

I have also developed a loving and forgiving relationship with my father as a result of my daily emotional exercises. I realized that his father wounded him in the same way he wounded me. To prevent myself from passing along those wounds to my children, I have sweated from my eyes a lot over the years, and my emotional workouts have challenged me through my pain. But overcoming the barriers and seeing the results has made it well worth the effort.

SOMETIMES IT TAKES BEING HIT BY A TREE

I never knew how much my seventy-year-old dad cared about me until a few winters ago when we gathered firewood in the forest behind our ranch. He began his own journey toward healing after my grandfather died. Today, I feel fortunate to spend time with him.

We rode out to the forest on my old snowmobile, towing a chainsaw and axe in a makeshift trailer attached to a pair of skis. We settled on a dead tree dried by the sun, ready to burn. One limb had broken off in the wind and dangled precariously, just above our heads. Without ladder, rope or forethought, we agreed to pull the limb out of the tree, so I pulled it over about twenty feet and let it go like a pendulum. I ran as it came loose. Unfortunately, I ran in the direction it fell. The broken limb struck my head and shoulders, knocking me to the ground. Barely conscious, I heard

> *Becoming emotionally fit is the best way to avoid the crises we bring on ourselves.*

20

my father running over to me. "David! Oh, my David. Oh, God! My David."

Blood covered the side of my head and seemed to be draining from my ear. My father thought I was dying. He wept at my side, not strong enough to carry me, saying my name over and over. What a moment! I wanted to lie there, feigning unconsciousness, listening to him grieve, listening to his words communicating his love. It was a healing moment.

Instead, I reassured him that all was okay and then dragged myself back to the snowmobile and told him to get on—he was in no condition to drive! I steered through the snowdrifts toward the house, fighting unconsciousness all the way. Fortunately, I only had the wind knocked out of me. The wound on my head was just a graze. I am glad this incident happened though, because it gave my father and me an opportunity to be real, to be honest, to express our true feelings for each other.

If only we men could learn to be real without the pain of an accident, a life-threatening illness or some other major crisis. It is too bad we will not risk connecting with those we truly care about, to express our love freely, our devotion, our commitment, our fears and concerns.

Sometimes we just have to be hit by a tree.

If you practice the exercises in this book, those moments of real connection will come easier. You will not need a crisis to bring them on, because emotional fitness leads to authenticity. Becoming emotionally fit is the best way to avoid the crises we bring on ourselves.

WORKING OUT

If you are a couch potato or one who likes to second-guess players from the sidelines, then emotional fitness is not for you. If you want to win in the game of life, you will have to prepare emotionally so that you can excel. In truth, your well being and that of your family depends on it. Emotional fitness is not about showing off or building emotional muscles so that you can compete on your good looks alone. It is about training to win in life.

Passion drives us to better ourselves. We need to love playing our position. How is your track record as a husband? Father? Community leader? As a boy, I did not like team sports. But I have learned that my family is the most important team on which I will play. I am the quarterback. That means I have the responsibility to make sure my team is winning.

When I work out, I sweat. If I do not, I know I am not working hard enough. Sometimes, overcoming emotional pain can be much harder than physical pain, and I have to *sweat from my eyes*. This is not something to fear. However, a lack of tears can signify that I am emotionally blocked. Too many tears can also indicate I am in bad shape.

Just as there is no quick way to lose weight or become physically fit, there are no quick paths to emotional fitness. This book lays out a short-term and a long-term plan that will promote your overall emotional health and help you build character and integrity. If you practice consistently just a few of the exercises presented, your emotional health and character will improve, and you will be on your way to leaving a positive legacy. You will also feel great, too!

Emotional change starts with committing to a course of action and then taking one step at a time. Just like an athlete, you must focus on every aspect of the game to hone your skills. It is hard work, but the payoff is worth it.

Are you ready to start?

PART I: DISCOVERING THE ZONES

CHAPTER 1:

SELF-ASSESSMENT

A LOOK IN THE MIRROR

New Year's Day usually arrives with a vengeance. I have over-indulged in eggnog, turkey and trimmings, cookies, cakes, and drinks throughout the holidays. The scale's digital readout displays numbers I have never seen before, and I need to let my belt out a couple of notches. I grab my waist. *Where did this spare tire come from? That is it! I'm going to join an exercise club, cut back on eating, and lose some weight.*

Sound familiar?

Other than the annual New Year's trek to the gym, it usually takes a crisis to make us start a workout routine. Some of us ignore subtler hints that we are out of shape, such as breathing hard after walking up a small hill. Others will not change lifestyles until a doctor warns, "Your cholesterol and blood pressure are too high. You need to start exercising." Sadly, some men will not pay attention to even the direst warnings. They wait until *after* the first heart attack—if they survive. Then they head to the gym on wobbly legs, feeling chastened and vowing never to neglect health and fitness again.

Obviously, it is far better to diet and exercise while you are still reasonably healthy. The same principle applies to your emotional health. What does an emotional heart attack look like? A divorce? A runaway teenager? Getting fired? Why wait until after your life unravels before you work on your emotions? Why not be honest about your emotional health right now?

Looking in the mirror is one way to assess your physical health, although, obviously, it does not tell the entire story. You cannot see your emotional self in a normal mirror, but there is a mirror into which you can look to assess your emotional well being.

THE THREE-SIXTY

In leadership coaching circles, a *three-sixty* is one technique used to help people look at themselves. Just as 360 degrees make up a circle, this method gives us a rounded view from every perspective. We are able to see ourselves the way others view us. On page 198 of this book is a survey I have developed entitled *The Emotional Mirror Survey—"What I See"*™. It takes about twenty minutes to fill out.

A couple pages later, you will also find a second survey called *The Emotional Mirror Survey—"What Others See"*™. Choose people who have seen you at your best and worst to fill this one out, and ask for an honest assessment. Do not be afraid of what you might learn about yourself. If you become defensive, you will be unable to listen. Many of us perceive feedback as personal criticism yet have little idea of how we are coming across. The truth may be painful, but the pain of an emotional heart attack is much worse than facing your emotional weaknesses and strengthening them safely.

If you do not know about or understand your feelings, now is the time to discover them. Yes, you may have to face emotions such as anger or resentment. But pretending they do not exist numbs and robs you of the joys that can be yours as your emotional fitness improves. You can turn yourself into a better person starting now, using the measurement tools and exercise routines in this book. If you complete the surveys now and again in three to six months, you will see positive changes. Trust me, it is worth the effort.

On my web site, www.sweatingfromyoureyes.com, you will find additional help and information. You can fill in your survey answers, and we will calculate your results. Friends, coworkers, and family can log on, submit your name, fill out a survey about you, and then we will compile their results, too. This will give you a 360-degree assessment of your emotional strength and fitness. I will send you a personal and confidential report, highlighting areas that need special attention. If you do not have computer access and do not want to write in this book, you have permission to make enough copies of *The Emotional Mirror Surveys* for personal use.

If, however, you plan on writing in this book or you want to photocopy the survey, then complete it and copy the totals into the appropriate quadrants in the box below. Do the same with the sum totals for the surveys from family and friends. In the next chapter, you will learn what your scores mean.

The Emotional Zones

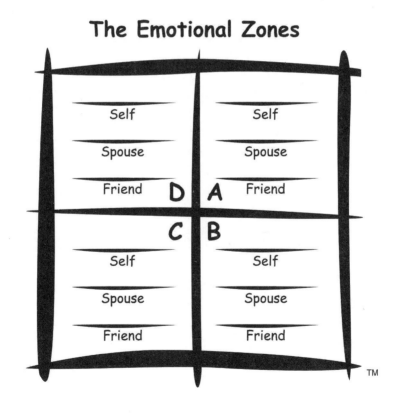

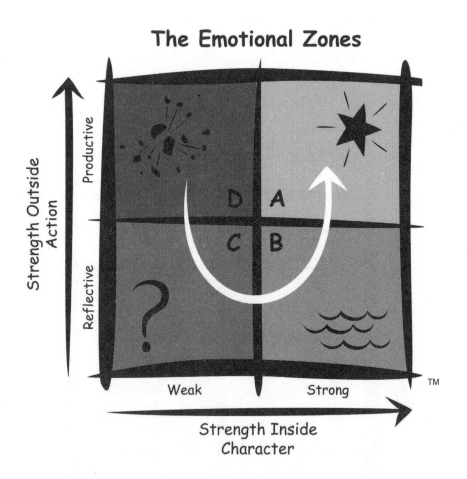

The Emotional Zones

CHAPTER 2:

THE ZONES

A SIMPLE TOOL

If you have ever played baseball, undoubtedly, you have been told to "Keep your eye on the ball." This little phrase can make the difference between a strikeout and a home run. As in baseball, in life, the simplest advice and solutions usually work best.

In keeping with this principle, I have developed a tool that helps explain your emotional make-up in an easy-to-understand model. The survey in which you entered your scores contains a box with four quadrants labeled A, B, C, and D. I call this tool "the Zones."

The Zones are both a diagnostic and a dynamic tool. As a diagnostic tool, they give you a snapshot of your emotional fitness as indicated by your scores on the surveys. The Zones then become a dynamic tool where you work out your emotions so that change takes place. In other words, no matter what the surveys say about you now, you are not bound to any one zone. The mirror never lies, but what you put before it can change.

First we will look at the Zones as a diagnostic tool. Later, I will explain how to use them as a dynamic tool. You will also learn how to use a "Zone check" in the same way you might take your pulse during an aerobics workout.

The scores from your surveys are plotted in the four zones. Note that the A-Zone is in the top right. Moving clockwise you will find B, C, and D.

The Emotional Zones

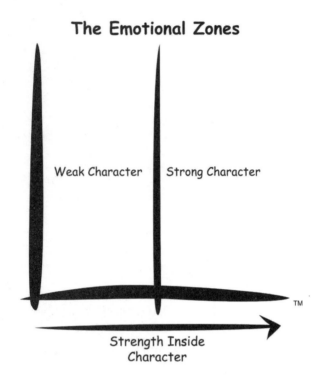

Weak Character   Strong Character

™

Strength Inside
Character

The horizontal scale rates your inner strength or character. The zones on the right side of this scale, A and B, denote strong character. These are the ones to aim for when developing emotional fitness. They mean you are "strong on the inside." The zones on the left, D and C, indicate weak character and low emotional fitness. These represent being "weak on inside."

The vertical scale rates your external strength or productivity. The zones above the horizontal mid-line are the *productive zones*, A and D. They reflect your "ability to do." A and D-Zone men get things done. They are "strong on the outside." The zones below the horizontal mid-line are the *reflective zones* and mirror your "ability to be." B and C are low productivity zones. They indicate "weakness on the outside." The B-Zone, however, is also a place of positive internal reflection when it is entered by choice. In fact, entering the B-Zone or *Being Zone* voluntarily is one of the best character-building exercises you can do. The C-Zone is a place of weakness inside and out. We all spent some time there even though we do not like to admit it.

The Emotional Zones

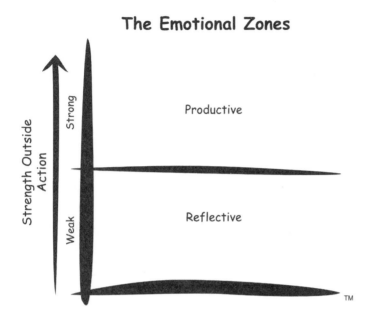

The Emotional Zones

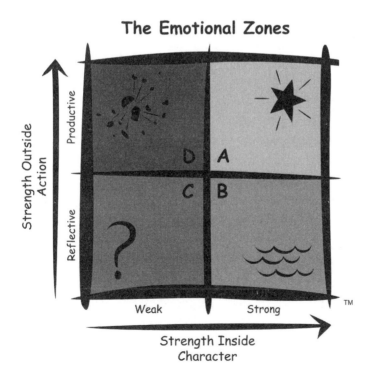

Ultimately, your goal is to spend most of your life in the A-Zone, where you are high in productivity and character, supported by quality time in the B-Zone to build and maintain that character.

THE D-ZONE

If you scored high in quadrant D, you are strong on the outside but weak inside. Your outer strength makes you task-oriented, and you can be counted on to accomplish a great deal. Inside, though, you are weak. This is the *Destructive Zone,* the zone of hidden, explosive anger.

Living in the D-Zone, you may be unaware of your anger. Or you may be keenly aware of it and like the feeling of power it provides. When you explode, you forget about it as soon as you have "let 'er rip." Unfortunately, the people you love cannot forget your anger so easily. Neither can your employees or co-workers. You have created a disaster zone with many casualties and much collateral damage to these relationships.

> *Living in the D-Zone, you may be unaware of your anger. Or you may be keenly aware of it and like the feeling of power it gives you.*

Maybe someone at the brunt of your explosive rage has filled out your survey to let you know that you are in the *Destructive Zone.* They are asking you to take a long look in your emotional mirror. You have had the guts to go this far, so keep going. Change is possible, and you can find healthy ways to deal with your anger without unleashing it on those around you.

A man who lives in the D-Zone is territorial and quick to take offense if someone crosses him or messes with his possessions. He rarely sees another's viewpoint or perspective. It is his way or the highway. He is quick to tell people what he thinks, especially those who are not on his side. Rarely does he solicit feedback, and if someone disagrees with him, "that's tough."

If you live in the *Destructive Zone,* you may be an angry tyrant at home, making your spouse and children tread lightly, afraid of upsetting you. As a D-Zone man, you tend to have limited emotional range and can be emotionally numb or feel various shades of irritation, annoyance, anger, and full-blown rage. Tenderness escapes you, but when someone hurts you, anger takes over quickly. Your expectations of others are high without you having to say or do anything. You are confrontational and sometimes look for a fight. Like your buddy in the *Can't Zone,* you see the world as a hostile place. But instead of passivity, you are bent on self-preservation, because you *know* that if you do not look after yourself, no one else will. You fear vulnerability, because vulnerability spells W-E-A-K-N-E-S-S.

Tony Soprano from *The Sopranos* TV series fits the D-Zone profile. He is strong on the outside but weak inside (though his wife and kids

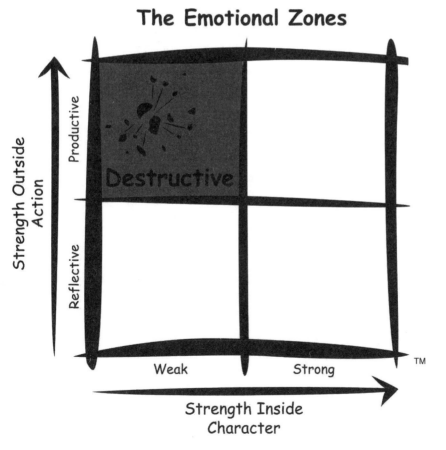

The Emotional Zones

Strength Outside
Action

Productive

Reflective

Destructive

Weak   Strong   ™

Strength Inside
Character

would also rate him in the C-Zone since they can push him around, even though his fellow mobsters are afraid of him). Another example is heavyweight boxer Mike Tyson. Once a champion inside the ring, he demonstrated a lack of emotional strength and character when he bit off Evander Holyfield's ear during a match and has since proven his lack of character in a consistent manner.

Living in the *Destructive Zone* causes stress-induced diseases, such as high blood pressure, heart attacks, and strokes. It also places you at risk for emotional disasters at home or work because of your anger. Your explosive rage shows that you do not handle stress very well.

THE C-ZONE

If you scored high in the C-Zone or *Can't Zone*, I applaud your honesty. If you asked others to fill out your survey, I commend your courage. It is painful to admit you live in a zone that is characterized by being weak inside and outside. It is the place of emotional weakness and low productivity. But do not beat yourself up. Just as it is possible to go from couch potato to fitness king, I assure you, it is possible to move out of the C-Zone into zones A and B.

The C-Zone is the *Can't Zone*, a place of passivity and inner frailty. Life seems dull and gray because you tend toward depression and discouragement. You comfort yourself and pump up your low self-image by harping on the faults of other people. Criticizing and judging are frequent pastimes, though you do not realize that these habits act like a boomerang, feeding your self-condemnation.

> *The C-Zone is the Can't Zone, a place of passivity and inner frailty.*

C-Zone men engage in compulsive introspection laced with self-loathing, defensive conversations, resentment, blame, and regrets. Instead of seeing failure as a learning experience, they use it to justify the status quo, whether it is a lousy job, bad habits or rotten relationships. A C-Zone man replays conversations in his mind, second-guesses himself,

34

and wishes he could change the past. He might fantasize about having that great comeback or putting a bully in his place. His stinging, sarcastic remarks stem from emotional weakness. He sees himself as a victim of circumstances, blaming others, bad luck, lousy weather or anything else for his failures and failed relationships. His attitude is, "Why should I bother? It will never make a difference."

If you are stuck in the *Can't Zone*, you perceive the world as a hostile place. You believe that people and circumstances conspire against you. That view contributes to your passivity and lack of motivation. You tend to magnify problems and blow things out of proportion. This makes you high maintenance for your loved ones; you demand a great deal from them.

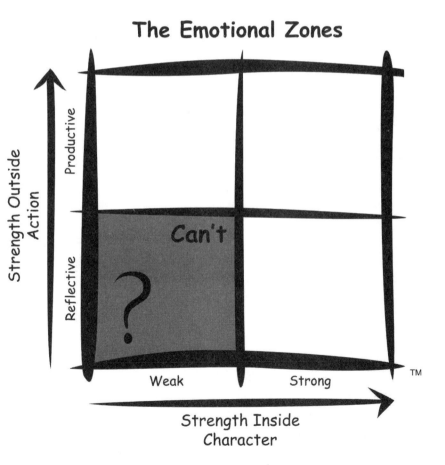

The Emotional Zones

You have a tendency to open up too quickly in friendships or relationships, a sure indicator of your inability to set boundaries. There are appropriate and inappropriate ways to talk about yourself, but you often choose wrong people and wrong times. You are easily abused or taken advantage of, confirming your pessimistic views and criticisms. Because you judge constantly, even your positive judgments prove wrong and come back to haunt you.

Homer Simpson is a *Can't Zone* personality. He is a nice, needy, childish, and passive guy. His wife, children, and co-workers push him around. The failing car salesman in the movie *Fargo* is another C-Zone man. He finds himself getting deeper and deeper into crime because he cannot say no. The *Can't Zone* man is like the proverbial couch potato, one who escapes into fantasy and resentment and abdicates his role as a loving husband and father.

If you are in the C-Zone, you may know you have bad habits that need to be addressed, but you feel stuck, overwhelmed or unable to change, and you hate yourself for being this way. However, if you resolve to practice just a few of my emotional exercises, you will be on the road to freedom. You can do it. I have been stuck in this zone many times, yet I have always been able to pull out of it. You can, too.

As a moody person, you find it difficult to accept feedback. That is why I am congratulating you for starting on the road to true growth and emotional health. Resist the impulse to strike back at those who have offered honest feedback, even if you find it difficult to hear right now.

Please do not hesitate to get professional help if you are depressed and have suicidal thoughts or a sense of despair and self-loathing. Getting help is a sign of strength, and it shows a willingness to take care of yourself.

THE B-ZONE

Like the A-Zone, the B-Zone or *Being Zone* represents emotional strength and strong character. It is on the negative end of the vertical scale that rates productivity, because it is a reflective rather than a productive zone. The B-Zone man is strong on the inside (where it counts) yet weak on the outside. While reflecting on his inner tendencies, he does not exhibit outer strength or accomplish tasks.

If you scored highest in the B-Zone, you are someone who looks for clarity. You are a seeker who wants answers to your questions. You express tenderness to those you love and are consistent with your principles. You are also more likely to seek the opinion of others before you make a decision.

The B-Zone man seeks advice and honest feedback from others because he knows he has blind spots. He is concerned about how he comes across because he wants to make sure he is communicating effectively. His desire to seek the opinions of others does not spring from a craving for approval or uncertainty about himself. It comes from a desire to grow into a better man.

The Emotional Zones

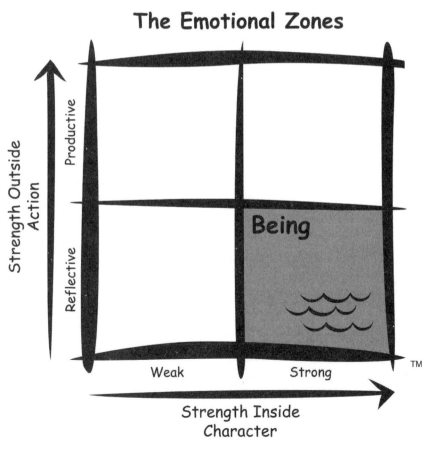

If you are a B-Zone man, you understand that people may take things you have said the wrong way. You might pick up the phone to clarify a previous conversation. You work hard at communicating effectively and listening well. You love to mull over ideas—thinking, talking, and reading about them. You place a major emphasis on self-development. In addition to finding honest friends whose opinions you trust, you also seek coaches or mentors who can help you.

The B-Zone man is strong on the inside.

You view painful life experiences as an opportunity to grow and wrestle with every experience to find meaning and truth. You can put yourself in others' shoes and, although you realize truth is objective, you recognize that others see different perspectives on it, and you strive to understand these perspectives

Lieutenant Columbo from the old mystery TV series exemplifies the *Being Zone* personality. He asks questions constantly and appears to have few answers. To criminals, he appears weak on the outside, but his internal reflection and questions eventually solve the case.

Too much time in the B-Zone, however, can lead to procrastination, and your pensiveness can become a weakness. I know *Being Zone* men who display tremendous character, have wonderful relationships with their family and friends but are not good at earning a living or keeping a team on track. They do not seem to get anything done. So, spending some time in the B-Zone is healthy. Just do not build your home there.

THE A-ZONE

If you scored highest in quadrant A—the *Actualizing Zone*—you are strong on the outside and strong on the inside. You exhibit emotional strength because you have both high character and high productivity. As a leader, you exude a sense of collected calm and trustworthiness on which others can rely. You set goals, accomplish them, and help others achieve theirs. Your consistency and priorities show that you walk your talk.

In the *Actualizing Zone*, your principles guide you, especially in the way you behave toward those who are weaker. Though capable of being loving and tender, you are no pushover.

Living in the A-Zone allows you to give others their space without condemnation. While you do not seek confrontation, you can defend yourself and your principles when necessary. You will not allow others to control you. Though able to discern right from wrong, you do not waste time judging others or using their shortcomings to make yourself feel superior. You can admit to areas that need improvement, and you are willing to work on them.

The Emotional Zones

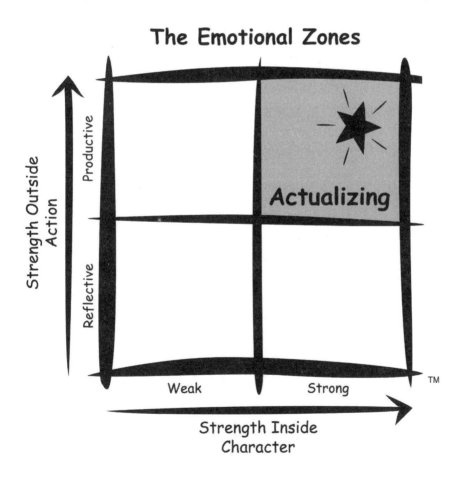

A-Zone men exude power that energizes everyone around them.

As an A-Zone man, you have confidence in yourself and your actions, and you do not need to brag. A-Zone men exude power that energizes everyone around them. They are like the star quarterback who knows how to make his team look great. He does not steal the limelight but gives credit to others. When he wins, everyone wins.

An A-Zone man considers comments and criticism objectively before reacting and maintains a balanced, realistic view of his strengths and weaknesses. He does not have to hide failures or become defensive about them. He knows when to be vulnerable and chooses carefully those to whom he reveals himself.

"Live and let live" is your motto. You pick your battles and understand when a tactical retreat is the best move. You are willing to confront negative behaviors and attitudes that block others from doing their best but rarely attack character. Your goal is to help others be their best, because it is the most effective way for a team to produce results or a family to find harmony. The Golden Rule of doing unto others guides your life, and you bring out the best in others, earning their respect and support.

Though firmly grounded in solid moral principles, you are a man who understands there are shades of gray, because we all have different perspectives on the same reality. You do not force others to see things your way but inspire them to be individuals.

An example of an *Actualizing Zone* man is William Wallace in the movie *Braveheart* or Atticus Finch in *To Kill a Mockingbird*. These men empower others; they build strong families and successful teams. They stand for principles and fight for justice even if it makes them unpopular. Men who live in the A-Zone build a strong positive legacy and leave a trail of goodness.

YOUR ZONE SCORES

Take time to understand the Zones. Your highest score indicates the one you and others believe you operate in most of the time. Your scores in the other quadrants reflect secondary emotional tendencies. Like your primary score, they represent snapshots in time, not a permanent diagnosis or final verdict on your life.

No one spends all of his or her time in one zone. You have scores for all four. That is because life is a dynamic process. It is easy to drift into the negative zones if you do not choose to work out your emotions on a regular basis. Compare your results to the ratings of friends and family and note any differences. Is there a discrepancy between the way you see yourself and the way others see you? Has someone given you a higher score in a zone than you have given yourself? If so, why do you think that is?

For instance, you may have rated yourself higher in the A-Zone than you really are, because you are not aware of how others see you or how you really feel. Many individuals tell me they are doing okay—they are in the A-Zone, being productive, and everything is fine. In truth, others see them in the D-Zone, because they have repressed anger leaking out and causing trouble. They do not feel they need to spend time in the *Being Zone*. At some point, however, they hit a wall and slip into D. In reaction, they hurt others.

Make it your objective to spend as little time as possible in Zones D and C. Commit to learning how to be productive without causing "collateral damage" in your relationships, and create a legacy of goodwill through high character action in the A-Zone.

THE TARGET ZONES

An emotionally healthy man moves with agility between Zones A and B, from the *Actualizing Zone* to the *Being Zone*, from a place of action and productivity to a place of reflection. An A-Zone man maintains his character by making regular trips to the B-Zone for reflection and ensures he has not slipped inadvertently into zone C or D.

Knowing exactly where you are is the starting point for any emotional growth, no matter how unpleasant it may be. That is a part of each zone's function: It gives you a paradigm to assess your thoughts and feelings so

The Emotional Zones

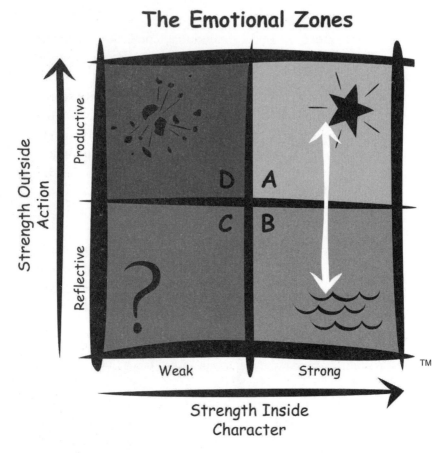

TM

you can discern and describe what is happening inside. Only when you face what is really going on inside can you change it.

If you have ever had a personal fitness trainer, he or she has probably told you to "listen to your body." Doing so can prevent injury, keep you from overextending yourself, and find the areas of weakness that need work. These same principles apply to your emotional workout. Listen to your body, your thoughts and feelings. Recognize when you feel something, whether anger, fear, anxiety or sadness. You might not pinpoint what is bothering you right away, but start paying attention. Observe how you feel when your boss berates you. Examine your feelings when your child defies you or your wife complains. What do you discover?

Learn to perceive your thoughts and feelings before they get out of control. Observing them objectively lessens their power to drive you

42

in a negative direction. You may discover a constant chatter of negative thoughts, as if someone is playing a tape recording over and over again. In the exercise portion of this book, you will learn how to resist these thoughts and replace them with good ones. These simple exercises in controlling what you think can have a huge positive impact on how you feel and how you behave. As a diagnostic tool, the Zones help you understand where you are now. You can choose how you want to think, feel, and act.

A DYNAMIC TOOL

Dynamic means "moving." Going somewhere. Fluid. Able to change. Using the Zones as a dynamic tool enables you to do just that: move,

The Emotional Zones

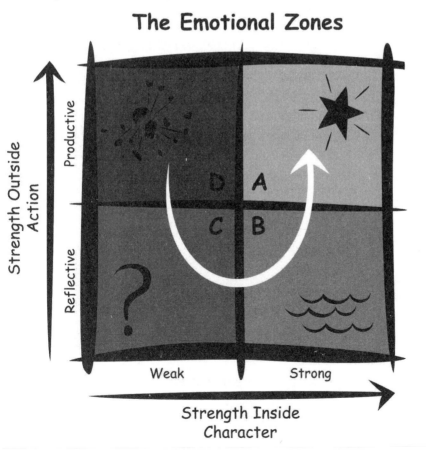

travel, flow, change, and become emotionally fit. Emotional fitness parallels physical fitness in that it is easier to maintain if you are already in peak condition. However, even for a person in top physical condition, bad habits can quickly deteriorate fitness and overall health. Time constraints may make you delay or miss your workouts. Soon you are hardly working out at all. Too many rich meals in a row, a change in circumstances, such as a new job, or a minor crisis, can throw you off your workout schedule. Without a concentrated effort, you can easily put on the weight and end up gasping when you climb a flight of stairs.

The same goes for emotional fitness. It is possible to slip from the *Actualizing Zone* into the *Destructive Zone* without even realizing it. But it does not work the other way around. Men in the D-Zone who understand

The Emotional Zones

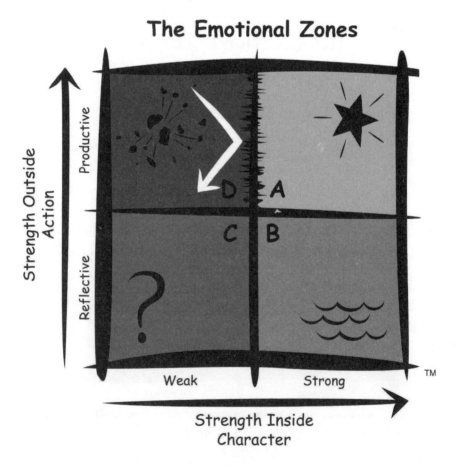

the benefits of the A-Zone often want an immediate transition. Unfortunately, the barrier between A and D is like a one-way membrane or a high-tech waterproof fabric that allows moisture to escape but prevents it from penetrating. (See diagram on page 44.)

> *At some point, we have picked up the message that that focusing on our emotions is for wimps. Do not play that game.*

If you are in the *Destructive Zone*, you will have to go through the C-Zone first. The road to change is counter-clockwise through the quadrants, from D to C to B to A. No one moves from directly from D to A. Men who see someone strong inside and outside think, "I want to be like him." The trouble is, no one becomes strong inside until they admit their inner weaknesses.

At some point, we have picked up the message that focusing on our emotions is for wimps. Do not play that game. The *Being Zone* is the door to the *Actualizing Zone*. You may think that is where the weaklings hang out. In fact, it is the place where men with inner strength renew themselves and grow stronger. The only way to maintain fitness in the A-Zone is to enter the B-Zone on a regular basis. *This* is where your emotional workouts take place. It is your inner gymnasium, your internal workout space. Here, you will improve your quality of life, gain energy, build stronger relationships, and find the strength to accomplish your goals.

Live dynamically. Be willing to change and take the necessary steps to move in the right direction. Remember, there is no "get out of jail free" card in either the D-Zone or the C-Zone. As you begin your journey toward emotional fitness, at times you will feel worse than you do now, because you are working out, and that always involves a certain degree of pain. Hang in there. Others may notice the positive changes even before you do.

In subsequent chapters, I will explain more about using the Zones as a dynamic tool for personality change, but first, let's zero in on the most problematic Zones—D and C.

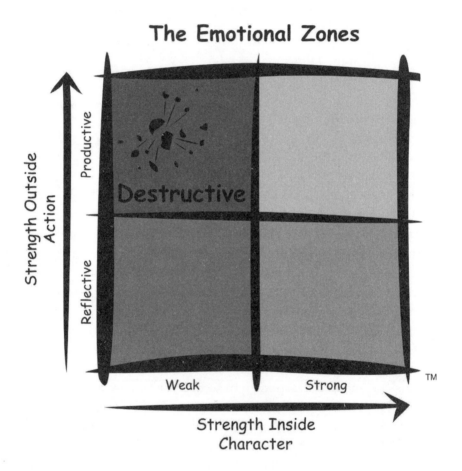

CHAPTER 3:

THE DESTRUCTIVE ZONE

Anger rules in the *Destructive Zone*. You may think you are controlling your anger because you blow up only occasionally. In fact, anger is controlling you.

It takes a tremendous amount of energy to keep the lid over your anger secure. Anger blocks our ability to perceive the other real feelings we may be experiencing, both positive and negative. It renders us unable to empathize, to listen genuinely to others or to see another's perspective. When we are continually angry, we are like boxers throwing wild punches. We leave ourselves open to counterattacks, which stir up greater levels of anger as we try to protect ourselves. Refusing to trust, we lunge and punch continually without discipline or control. This psychological battle can easily end in a heart attack or a stroke. It can fry the immune system. For some of us, the battle can become literally bloody.

It is unfortunate that our society grants men tacit permission to live in the *Destructive Zone*. For years, Hollywood films have celebrated the "angry man" who seeks vengeance on his enemies. We are encouraged to cheer and applaud such men rather than recognize them as the aberration of masculinity that they are. In addition, many outwardly strong men in leadership positions, including many fathers, are angry men who exert power to accomplish tasks or get their way. Often these macho men are the only role models we have had. When given a choice between becoming an angry, powerful guy who gets things done or a passive, outwardly weak man, most of us would rather have power, even if it is fueled by rage.

The D-Zone man's ability to throw his weight around may feel like freedom. But if he sits still long enough to examine what is really going on, he will see that his mind is filled with contempt, criticism, blame, negative self-talk, resentment, and excuses. The *Destructive Zone* is a maze of negativity.

It is difficult for a D-Zone man to stop justifying his anger. If you are one of them, it is easy to blame others for making you angry. It is tempting to deny the angry nature you have cultivated. In fact, you may have become addicted to anger, dependent on the rush of energy it provides.

Anger, however, is a secondary emotion. It is a cloak for anxiety and fear. It is a protective emotion that kicks in without warning, releasing adrenaline and other chemicals into our system when we feel threatened. This hormonal cocktail dulls sensitivity and creates emotional tunnel vision, making it difficult to get out of the angry state.

One of the things we humans share with animals is what psychologists call the "fight-or-flight" syndrome. We fight or flee in response to stress. That means fear and anger are linked closely in our psyches. Anger can mask deep-seated fear and keep us in denial. Those of us stuck in this zone want an easy way out. We want someone to wave a magic wand and put us smack into the *Actualizing Zone*. We often fantasize about how we would be in the A-Zone if everyone around us would stop doing what annoys us. Pride blocks us from examining the weakness hiding behind our anger. We would rather live in denial than admit it is us who are weak, not others.

When you start to resist your anger (not suppress it—suppression never works), you will go through stages where you will feel worse than you did before starting your workouts. That is okay. You are beginning to discover the hidden feelings behind your rage. You will move into the *Can't Zone*—a scary place to be—but the road to the A-Zone and emotional health leads this way. You can compare the pain you feel from working out your anger to the soreness that accompanies your first gym visits after a long time of resting on the couch.

There are genuine reasons to be angry. Someone may have deliberately offended or undermined you. However, in the D-Zone, sometimes it is difficult to determine whether you have a real reason to be angry, since you have become addicted to the feeling. Emotionally fit people use their anger as an indication that something is wrong, but they are careful to keep their behavior in check. They do not throw dumbbells at the person with whom they are angry. They take time to calm down so they can understand the precise problem without "seeing red." If you are feeling angry, a pause before you act will help discern whether you have a legitimate reason to be angry and, if so, what reasonable steps you can take in response.

You may have rated yourself high in the D-Zone or your friends and family may have rated you high there. In spite of your scores, however, you may feel like you are doing all right. Perhaps you have handled major stress in your life like a divorce or financial crisis without falling apart. You may think you are strong emotionally, because you have survived intact.

Emotionally fit people use their anger as an indication that something is wrong, but they are careful to keep their behavior in check.

As men, we tend to handle life's big problems a lot better than everyday ones. For instance, how do you react when someone tailgates you, cuts you off in traffic or makes an obscene gesture at you? What you choose to do with your everyday anger can lead to an emotional and/or physical breakdown when bigger stresses hit. If you have experienced a divorce, been fired or lost a business, think about how you handled the little moments. Could your anger toward small things have played a role in alienating your spouse, children or co-workers?

Here is your first emotional exercise: When you feel angry over something little, like the slowpoke driving in the fast lane, acknowledge it. Sense that emotion. Do not pretend the feeling is not there. But do not take immediate action either. Resist the temptation to get high off your anger rush. Deal with your anger by admitting it to yourself. Observe it without judging or self-condemnation. Then resist it by not allowing it to color your perception. When you are angry, you may see things in black-and-white terms and make "always-or-never" statements to yourself or those you love. "You are always such a slob!" you might scream at your teenager when he or she leaves something lying around. Or you might yell, "Why do you have to be so stupid?" when your son leaves a toy truck in the middle of the stairs.

> *When you are angry, you may see things in black-and-white terms and make "always-or-never" statements to yourself or those you love.*

When you are angry, black-and white thinking replaces calm, objective, principled rational thought that is available to guide you even when your feelings fluctuate. In black-and-white mode, you might say to your kids, "Why can't you do anything right?" when, of course, that is not true. Damaging words like those have devastating consequences for your children. Once you have identified and observed your anger, it is critical to handle yourself correctly. This is where you start bench pressing, using it as resistance.

VENTING ANGER

Some people believe that all anger needs to be released. They advise you to vent, to scream, beat up a pillow or hit a punching bag. They say it is dangerous to hold feelings in. They tell you to take out your anger on an inanimate object so you avoid confrontations that can lead to being fired, losing a valued employee or harming a loved one. As my kids would say, "That's old school."

Anger is not like a gas that builds pressure until it needs to be vented into the atmosphere. Holding onto this model will lead you to believe that you have no choice but to fly off the handle. Unfortunately, it is usually someone weaker like your children or even your dog that bears the brunt. Anger does not build up. In fact, blowing up can multiply it.

Anger is a method of self-protection, a way to control and manipulate others. We hide behind its force field when we are hurt inside, using it to deny our inner pain. When we observe and acknowledge it, we can begin to understand its root causes and choose to act appropriately so that our anger dissipates without the need to lash out.

Venting anger only cultivates an angry nature. Allowing anger to diffuse prevents it from becoming an addiction and stops you from developing a rage-based character. Here is another exercise for you to try: Think of a time when you have blown up at someone and vented your anger on him or her. When venting, you made the person the object of your anger and blamed him or her for how you felt. Even if they had done something against you, your hostility indicates you were out of control. Continue reflecting on this incident. What was really fueling your anger? Self-protection? Self-justification? An emotional wound from the past? When you acknowledge the real cause of your anger, you diffuse its power. It governs your actions no longer. Then you can address what the person has done and deal with it in a positive way.

WHEN TO ACT

When my children were small, I would get upset with their occasional disobedience

> *Anger is a method of self-protection, a way to control and manipulate others. We hide behind its force field when we are hurt inside, using it to deny our inner pain.*

or childish mistakes. During my outbursts or immediately afterwards, I realized that my anger-fuelled actions hurt them. My outbursts fostered fear and insecurity and built walls around my children's hearts that could also defend them against my good intentions. An angry response does not correct behavior that needs changing. It makes the behavior worse. I am well aware of my father's detrimental anger towards me, and I did not want to pass that baggage on to my children. So I turned to Phil Geldart, a man I trust, a man who has shown admirable restraint and love for his children.

"Why can't I control my emotions?" I asked him one day. "I always lash out in anger, especially with those I love. I'm forever doing the things I don't want to do. Why can I exhibit self-control in public, in business meetings, and (usually) on the sports field, yet my anger surfaces on my home turf?"

In his classic, gracious way, Phil explained to me how he had learned to manage his anger. He taught me the concept of the *anger-action line*.

"We always act," he said, "but we usually act too late. Rarely do we act too early."

Then he showed me the chart on the following page. The line on the left side measures the level of anger. The line running from left to right across the bottom indicates elapsed time. When we see something we do not like, we feel our anger starting to brew.

"It is important to take action before anger grows exponentially, when controlling it would be far more difficult, if not impossible," he said. Phil also suggested that I give my children clear and reasonable instructions. I needed to let them know what behavior I expected and the consequences of disobedience.

"We always act," he said, "but we usually act too late. Rarely do we act too early."

By making an effort to stay in touch with my feelings and choosing not to vent my anger, I learned to discipline my children without harming them. Many dads strike out in frustration and damage their children's character development rather than correcting them calmly. Disciplining out of anger harms the child, but that does not mean all forms of discipline are negative.

Unfortunately, we are inconsistent. One day, we are in a good mood and do not care if the dishes are washed or homework is finished. Then, when they come home with a "D" on their report cards, we blow our stacks.

Acting at the first signs of anger, coupled with setting a clear line of expectations, works well for those who can feel their anger coming on. But this model does not work for those of us who have developed an angry nature of which we are completely unaware.

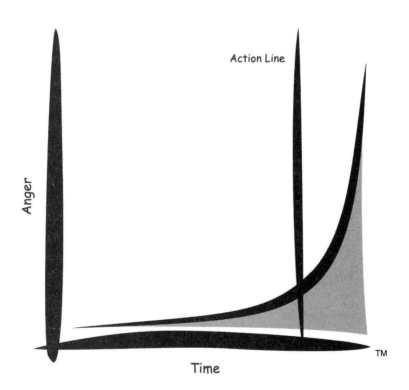

WHEN ANGER GRIPS YOU

You may be someone who lives in a perpetual state of anger. If so, your anger diagram probably looks something like the one on the following page.

When anger boils continually at a high rate, there is no appropriate place for an action line. Any problem, such as a child who refuses to go to bed on time, could trigger an angry response that is way out of proportion to the offence. Even an accident, such as a small child spilling milk, can make you shout or slam your fist on the table.

If you are aware of your capacity for rage and try to contain it so you do not hurt others, you may have developed many strategies for preventing angry outbursts. You try to stuff down your anger, put a lid on your emotions, and fasten it down so your negative feelings will not escape. You attempt to live above the anger line. You may be so successful at this that you have persuaded yourself that you are not angry. Many of us are used to living with D-Zone anger and think it is normal.

That kind of suppression has a price. If you do not feel your anger, you will not feel much else either. Denying anger compromises your other feelings and dulls your emotional sensitivity. If you are angry in response to pressure, crisis, misplaced wallets, scattered toys, and your wife's menstrual cycles, you become desensitized to other emotions. You will not experience joy, love, comfort, peace, and the pleasures of everyday life.

If you are emotionally numb, trying to cap the simmering volcano inside of you, then take your first step toward emotional fitness by acknowledging your anger. Do not release it. Do not start spewing lava. Just admit the way it feels in your gut. Be careful not to lapse into the comfort of blaming others. You need to "own," take responsibility for your emotions as well as your actions. No more blame game.

Denying anger compromises your other feelings and dulls your emotional sensitivity.

The next step is to examine what created your anger. Ask yourself, "Why am I angry? What am I scared of? What is creating anxiety? How can I choose to deal with these emotions consciously in positive ways without allowing my anger to take over?" The key is to identify why your feelings surfaced and understand your role in any conflict so you can change your behavior. Finally, you need to take appropriate steps to correct the person or the problem. Sometimes you cannot change whatever it is that upsets you. But, using the exercises in this book, you can learn how to control your response to provocation. Note that I said, "response." If you work out emotionally, you will no longer react to stress like a puppet.

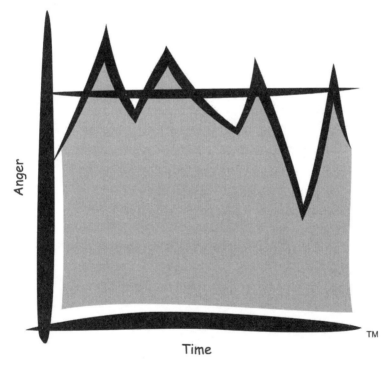

MOVING OUT

For men, moving out of the *Destructive Zone* is extremely difficult, because D-Zone behavior is often the only model of strength and manliness we have. We have come to think of that state as normal. I have news for you: It isn't. If you want to move out, the first step is to identify that you are stuck here. Second, acknowledge your need to change. Third, give yourself permission to move from perceived strength to perceived weakness—a state of vulnerability. Fourth, choose to change by shedding your outward pose of strength.

Being vulnerable is a tough thing to do. It is taboo for most men. "I can't do it; I need help," are difficult words to utter. However, being vulnerable leads to listening, understanding, learning, and communicating more effectively.

Many of our business and sports role models are trapped in the D-Zone. An athlete may perform superbly on the court or the ice, but whenever he gets into the soft stuff, he says, "That's not for me."

The Emotional Zones

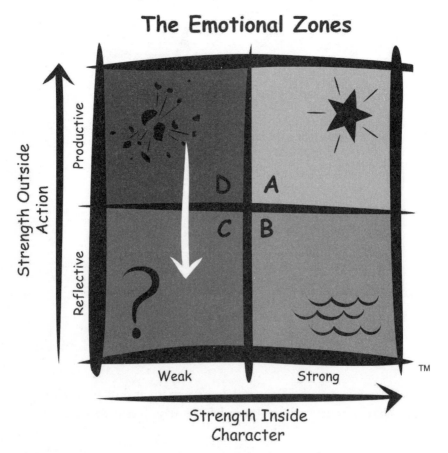

Similarly, a successful businessman may be angry and hurting and not know how to deal with his negative feelings.

Bound by their inner rage and distress, D-Zone men do not believe they have permission to acknowledge any inner weakness. The athlete's physical prowess and the businessman's high-powered schedule temporarily shield them from dealing with their inner turmoil. If a man is highly successful, it can be even harder for him to get out of the D-Zone trap.

If anyone understands how hard it is to get out of the D-Zone, it is Paul Henderson. In Canada, Henderson is a sports icon. In the last game of the 1972 Canada/Soviet All-Star hockey series, he scored the winning goal. Almost everyone in Canada has either watched the series on television or witnessed what has been dubbed "the goal of the century" in a replay.

As Paul Henderson explains in his personal story, found on the web site www.powertochange.com, that winning goal did not mean he had conquered his inner turmoil. He admits that he experienced "restlessness, a discontentment at the center of my being that I could not ignore. I was angry, bitter, and frustrated, and there were things about my life I did not know how to handle." He turned to alcohol as a solution.

> *Being vulnerable leads to listening, understanding, learning, and communicating more effectively.*

"I started drinking as a way to soothe the pain. I think if you are frustrated and angry, you look for a way out. You get with the boys and you try to 'make merry,' but you wake up the next morning, and it is there again."

Paul continued trying to solve his problems this way until a friend talked to him about taking care of his soul. At that point, he realized he "had never really looked at himself on the inside."

Now Paul is a motivational speaker to men and women in positions of leadership all over North America. I have heard him tell his inspiring story of change and have come to know him personally. In doing research for this book, I interviewed him to find out how he had overcome the D-Zone mind-set.

What I discovered is that Paul makes a practice of self-examination and reflection. He knows how to move from the *Destructive Zone* to the *Can't Zone*, then into the *Being Zone* until he can live in the *Actualizing Zone*. He is an example of someone who has practiced the exercises and principles found in this book. One of those principles is seeking the input of others to find out where you need to change. That is something else at which Paul is a pro.

"Few people do a very good job of self assessment—assessing their weaknesses—without the input of others," Paul says. He relies on his staff members to hold him accountable. "I told them, 'If I am going to be a better leader, you have got to tell me when I have hurt your feelings, when I have handled myself in a way that is unbecoming or did not show emotional intelligence.'

"I need feedback from others when I've hurt them. In the past, I've hurt people, and I didn't even realize I'd done it. You can become so 'D' you become oblivious. In the D-Zone, it is easy to get directive and authoritative at the wrong times. You get so task-oriented, and you think everyone else is there, too."

As those who have lived in the D-Zone for any length of time know, all you care about at that point is keeping everyone in line and moving forward to win. Paul found that when he sought needed input and took time to reflect upon it, he would go back and make amends to the people he had hurt.

If you have made the effort to hand out the survey, you have taken the first step toward getting to that crucial input. The underlying weakness of the *Destructive Zone* needs to be disclosed. The outer strength camouflaging inner weakness needs to be shed so you can build true inner strength. To do this, you need to go through the C-Zone.

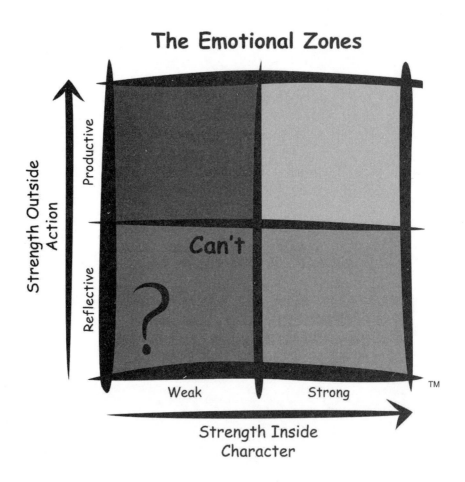

The Emotional Zones

CHAPTER 4:

THE CAN'T ZONE

A NEGATIVE SELF-IMAGE

In the C-Zone or *Can't Zone*, fear—often expressed as anxiety—predominates. These feelings trap you in a victim mentality and render you passive.

A man who dwells in the C-Zone hates anger and fears confrontation, because he does not want to imitate the angry men or women around him. These traits lead to an overwhelming sense of powerlessness, which breeds other negative feelings.

If you are in the C-Zone, you may feel morally superior to angry D-Zone men whom you blame for upsetting you and preventing you from achieving your goals. You may console yourself with the reassurance that you are not like the angry tyrants who make your life miserable. In response to the rage of others that has damaged you, you hate anger so much that you would rather be a victim than a victimizer. You assume you have no alternative. This is typical black-and-white, C-Zone thinking.

Unconsciously, you may also opt for depression and anxiety, because these are more acceptable feelings to you than rage, which does not fit with your nice-guy image. However, when you probe these feelings, you might uncover explosive rage buried

The mind tricks in the C-Zone can be subtle.

underneath deep hurt. Because you find anger unacceptable, you may turn it inward and find yourself full of self-loathing. If left unchecked, this self-directed rage could turn into suicidal thoughts.

In the C-Zone, we may experience a seesaw of hating ourselves then feeling sorry for ourselves. The mind tricks in the C-Zone can be subtle. If these thoughts and feelings are left unacknowledged and you do not work out emotionally, they can endanger your marriage and your long-term mental and physical health.

PRIDE

Despite his success as a star NHL player and his goal of the century, Paul Henderson knows what it is like to be in the C-Zone.

"I used to beat myself up. I had a standard of perfection and unrealistic expectations of myself. When you continually beat yourself up because of not doing something, that reverts to pride. Once you get to a certain point and you move into despondency, that is pride."

It might be surprising to discover that pride is a root cause of much of the self-loathing in the *Can't Zone*. Paul Henderson puts his finger right on the culprit—perfectionism, a form of pride. People who hate themselves often have a perfectionist streak, imposing impossibly high standards on themselves. If you take the time to reflect and examine yourself, you will discover that perfectionism and self-inflicted punishment go hand in hand. In your pride, you are playing judge and executioner on yourself. Though it is important to take responsibility for your shortcomings, you do not have to punish yourself for failing to meet your own impossible standards. It will not accomplish anything except to deepen your discouragement and bury you further in the *Can't Zone*.

Pride is also at the root of your tendency to blame others. It also allows you to cultivate your sense of victimization. You can feel proud and morally superior if your failures are the "fault" of other people.

FEAR

It may sound silly to say this, but one of the most frightening things you will ever confront is your fear. Though some people love the artificial fear generated by movies or thrill rides, the real thing is humiliating. We hate feeling endangered, helpless, and out of control.

The first step in dealing with fear is to recognize its control over your life. You do not have to wallow in it or magnify it, but give yourself permission to experience it. Try not to fear your fear. And ask yourself: Is the object of your fear real or imaginary?

The second step is to recognize that you do not have to act on your fear. Calmly observe and understand your reactions to whatever you fear, then write out your thoughts and feelings in your journal or confide in a trusted friend. Doing either of these things can be enough to dissipate fear and anxiety in a natural way.

The third step is to tell yourself: "It's okay to be afraid. I do not have to be perfect, and I can overcome my fear." If you give yourself permission to experience your feelings without kicking yourself in the butt, you will stand a much better chance of being set free.

Have you ever noticed that sometimes as soon as you feel fear or anxiety, you judge yourself? As soon as you do, condemnation, hatred, and various other self-inflicted punishments are added to the mix, driving you deeper into despair. If you slow down enough, you will notice that the voice inside your head that berates you may not be your voice at all. It may be the voice of your mother or father or someone who bullied you in your past. You may hate and punish yourself and vow to change. Sadly, the opposite happens. You create a negative cycle of emotion that keeps you chained in the C-Zone. Worse, you may finally blow your stack and go off into the D-Zone, where your hatred boils over onto others.

Paul Henderson recalls being ten or eleven years old and afraid of the dark. He never dared to share that fear with anyone.

"I was told to suck it up and be a real man. I was taught that real men don't cry. Real men are courageous. I was afraid of the dark, but I didn't want to admit it, because if I told someone, that would have been a weakness.

"I should have been told as a little guy that I was going to have some fears. As a little guy, courage is something you learn. You aren't born with it; you have to develop it."

SHAME

Sometimes, shame counterfeits the genuine conviction we feel when our conscience bothers us. If you have a guilty conscience, you need to listen to what it is telling you and let it guide you to a solution.

How can you tell the difference between guilt and shame in your life? Real guilt points to something specific, whereas shame merely condemns you as a failure. Step back and take an objective look at what you are doing. If you quiet yourself and ask, "What is it that I need to see? What am I doing wrong?" you will usually find a specific answer, a reason for feeling guilty.

When you get your answer, follow through. Admitting or disclosing to someone you trust is a great help. Within the quietness of your mind, you can also confess to God and then unburden yourself by writing in your journal. After resolving to turn away from doing whatever is causing your guilt, determine to make amends to anyone you have offended.

Sometimes when we have done all of these things, we still feel ashamed. Some of us walk around with a continual feeling of shame, as if nothing we can do will ever be good enough. We feel we are so deeply flawed that we could not bear to let anyone see what we are really like inside.

Thousands of men feel shamed this way but are afraid to admit it. Why do you feel shame? Does your past haunt you? Family secrets (things you cannot talk about), abuse by an authority figure, and things you may have done or said are all avenues for shame to enter into your life. Shame makes you feel like less of a man. Because of your past, you feel that somehow you are different from other men and an object of contempt. You feel bad about yourself and have low self-esteem.

If you have done all that is necessary to alleviate genuine guilt and you still feel shame, here are some other things you can do: Start with honesty. Admit that your shame renders you powerless. Doing so will transform the *Can't Zone* into the *Change Zone* as you reflect on your state of mind without judging yourself. You are resisting shame, one of the resistance exercises I will discuss in a subsequent chapter.

If you can pinpoint experiences that have left you with a sense of shame, contemplate them. For example, if you came from an abusive home or someone in a position of trust abused you sexually, resist taking responsibility for what happened. Fight against finding ways to blame yourself. *You did nothing wrong.* As you reflect, you can begin to adjust your behavior by telling yourself, "I can change. I am not the behavior I'm ashamed of." Soon, you will feel the sense of shame begin to lift.

If, however, you still feel a persistent sense of shame after you have done the workout, seek out a professional counselor or a trusted religious leader in your spiritual tradition. You can be free of shame, condemnation, feelings of unworthiness, and undefined but overwhelming guilt. Remember that shame is a blanket state of mind that is part of the murky C-Zone maze. Resist shame. Disagree with it. But if you suspect there is a true source of guilt, make sure you follow your conscience and bring your behavior in line with your principles of right and wrong.

BURIED RAGE

If you live in the C-Zone, you might imagine yourself as a victimized nice guy. You might be so afraid of experiencing anger that you completely deny its existence and check out of life to avoid confrontation. You become passive and accommodating at the expense of your emotional health.

Once you peel away your nice guy image, however, you will discover a mother lode of rage and hurt buried underneath your anxiety and fear. When you allow yourself to experience that rage, you will be tempted to enjoy the sense of power that comes with it. You might enjoy playing the role of an intimidator or victimizer for a change. You might also find it exhilarating to see other people shaking in their boots when you demand your rights or lower the boom on them.

Revenge may feel sweet, but in reality, you have merely moved from the C-Zone into the D-Zone—from one zone of weakness to another.

You may think you feel better, but those around you will suffer the consequences of your fleeting sense of rage-fuelled well being.

Some of us who fall into the C-Zone will do anything to get out. That is why it is important to work out in the *Being Zone* so you will not follow the natural tendencies of emotional weakness and victimize your loved ones.

For example, I was leading a men's group, trying to show the members that it is okay to be vulnerable. I disclosed a story of failure in my life from twenty years ago to show a fellow member of the group that I identified with his issues. "I've been there before, and know what it is like," I said, after revealing an example of Dave Loney in low-character mode.

Afterwards, for some reason, a guy in the group called me a word similar to "idiot," only not as kind. Even though I resisted taking the hit, something within me agreed with his assessment. "You are an idiot," I said to myself. Instead of identifying with the person I am now, I accepted and reaped the lie of that accusation. I slipped into C without even being aware of it. Keeping the smile and the eye contact, I ended our meeting in our usual way, with a short prayer. But I left in a C-Zone fog and arrived home in the D-Zone, where I took out my frustration on my wife and kids—all because I took a stupid remark to heart. A man can quickly slip from the A-Zone to either the C or D-Zone without being aware of it. And, for many of us, the trip to D starts in C.

As soon as we lose that *Being Zone* perspective and stop paying attention to our emotional and spiritual life, we fall back to our old selfish nature and into the D-Zone. Senseless, offhanded comments are exactly the sort of stimuli that can shove us there.

DEPRESSION

Anger turned inward, shame, and fear all contribute to depression. Depression is characterized by hopelessness, despondency, an inability to gain pleasure from life, emotional numbness, and feelings of worthlessness. Anxiety, a symptom of depression, is a form of fear. Another name for anxiety is worry. And worry feeds the cycle of negative thinking that leads to depression, creating more anxiety. We worry about our finances, our children, our health, our future. We think worrying shows our concern, when in reality we fear our lack of control over people and circumstances. Our outlook is negative.

In subsequent workout routines, I will show you how to overcome negative emotions through specific exercises. But first, I want to talk about proper reflection—the first step to removing negative feelings and behavior from your life.

COURSE CORRECTION

When people remain trapped in the negativity, passivity, and victim mentality of the *Can't Zone,* the characteristics of this quadrant become brush strokes in a personality portrait. Behind the emotional paralysis and ineffectiveness lies a mentality full of thoughts like, "I can't change," or "It's not my fault" or "If only…"

Remember: The Zones are not just a static diagnostic tool. They are also a dynamic tool. By using the word *static,* I am not referring to that crackling sound and fuzzy picture on your television set when you lose the signal. I mean not moving, still, stationary. Stuck. *Dynamic* means moving, changing—the opposite of static.

Previously, we learned that the road out of the *Destructive Zone* leads through the C-Zone. The underlying weakness of the *Destructive Zone* needs to be exposed, and the false outer strength that camouflages it needs to be shed. This allows inner strength to build. This type of disclosure happens in the C-Zone, which then becomes the *Change Zone,* a place of growth.

First, though, you need to identify that you have failed and not stay "down in the dumps." The more risks you take in your personal life, the greater your chance of failure. Do not let this hold you back.

I love to ski, whether downhill or cross-country. I have also learned to snowboard in the past few years. In these sports, one of the most important things to do when falling is to go with the motion and use the momentum to get back up and keep going. If you stiffen up, injuries can occur.

I do not think it is graceful to pick myself up from a still position on the snow and then sort out my tangled equipment. It is far better to roll and flip; doing whatever it takes to get back on two legs, pointing downhill. A correction like that has a way of getting onlookers in the chair lift to cheer instead of jeer. Use the momentum of failure to plant you right back on your feet again, moving forward. When you admit your C-Zone failures, you are using their momentum to get back up. It can now be called the *Courage Zone*, because it takes courage to face your weaknesses, correct them, and change.

THE CHANGE ZONE

Once you have decided to work out your emotions, the C-Zone becomes the *Change Zone*, the *Correction Zone*, and the meaningful starting point for permanent change in character.

If the Zones were a golf course, the C-Zone would be the sand trap that your golf ball must either cross or rise from if you are to finish each hole. You move out of the D-Zone, over the C-Zone sand trap, into the B-Zone (the fairway), and land, ultimately, on the putting green, the *Actualizing Zone*. If you get stuck in the sand trap (paralyzed by the negativity and passivity of the *Can't Zone*), you are living in a static mode. When you see the Zones as dynamic, you make sure your emotional life moves across or out of the sand trap with the properly applied technique.

A golfer cannot take practice swings in the sand trap. Once he approaches the ball, he has but one shot. All the practice swinging needs to be done outside the sand trap. In the same way, practicing your emotional sand trap exit strategy occurs best in the B-Zone. That is where you visualize the shot properly, the correct angles, and where you want the ball to go. Once in the C-Zone sand, it is all follow through—doing what you set out to do. Then the ball breaks free and rolls toward the green.

A pro makes hitting a ball out of a sand trap look easy. He has paid his dues in the pre-shot routine and in hours and hours of practice. You want to make your recovery from the sand traps of life look just as effortless. But having the skill to be strong on the inside and outside

The Emotional Zones

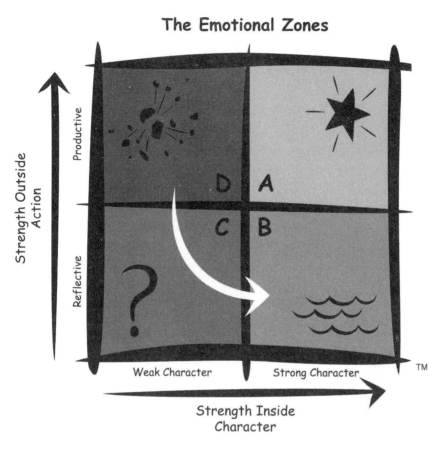

means you need to practice your pre-shot routines so that when crises come, you are ready.

The following is a journal entry I made while wallowing in the *Can't Zone*. You will see how I turned the *Can't Zone* into the *Change Zone* through proper reflection. It is not pretty, but I hope you will benefit from what I share.

A JOURNAL ENTRY: REALLY BUMMED

She comes home and opens a bottle of wine. I'm already halfway through my Scotch, having buried myself in my workshop over the barn to avoid confrontation upon her arrival. Funny how I do not want to answer the phone in the shop, knowing it is her, just to show her how it feels when countless others call and she doesn't pick it up.

I'm constantly finding fault in the way she approaches life. Yet when she speaks, when she writes, she seems so sound. I am not a part of her fairy tale world. I am not a figment of her imagination. She has great expectations for me. She says she wants simplicity, yet when I try for it, I almost always seem to fall short. "That is not what you were supposed to say or how you should have acted," she insinuates.

Often when we meet after being apart for a few hours, we'll size each other up, checking to see where we're both at. And we'll both know that neither of us is where the other wants us to be, so we adjust and fake it, just enough to help the other one feel a bit better.

Truth seems to evade us, for some reason. I guess it is because we really do not want to know it. I really do not want to live the rest of my life this way. I'm not really sure what to do about it though.

Notice how I am annoyed that my wife did not always answer the phone when friends called us? What was my response? I paid her back by not answering her calls while hiding in the workshop and drinking Scotch to numb my feelings.

In my journal, I acknowledged my habit of finding fault with her. At the same time, I noted feeling as though she was constantly finding fault with me. My judgments and criticisms of Cathy boomeranged back as criticisms and judgments of myself. I thought I could read her mind and then reacted negatively to what I *assumed* she was thinking.

When I wrote, "Truth seems to evade us" and made the blanket statement, "We don't want to know it," that we were "faking it," I engaged in black-and-white, either/or thinking. I blamed Cathy for "making" me feel like I did not measure up, when really those feelings were self-imposed. No one can "make" me feel anything. The use of the word *constantly* is a dead give away for black-and-white thinking. No one does anything "constantly" except breathe.

Now let's look at my next entry.

> *The Bible says to "Be transformed by the renewing of your mind"*
> *Romans 12:2). Let God turn you into a new person by changing*
> *the way you think. Treat her as you would treat your own body,*
> *care for her and love her unselfishly.*

Because I take my Christian faith seriously, I wrote down a verse from the Bible that outlined a principle I wanted to implement in my life. I reminded myself of the way I wanted to love and treat my wife. That was a good step to take and a good emotional exercise. Because I was in the *Can't Zone*, however, I resisted the positive side of the verse and used it to beat myself up for failing to meet these standards. One of the "stinking thinking" attributes of the *Can't Zone* is perfectionism. It usually manifests as, "If I can't do it perfectly, I might as well give up." My perfectionism tried to keep me in failure mode constantly.

My feelings and thoughts, still in negative territory, led me to entertain thoughts of divorce. But my principles made me reflect on the consequences. My journal entry continues:

> *What are the consequences of divorce? Loneliness, embittered*
> *kids, guilt, resentment, ongoing disputes.*
> *What would she gain? The freedom to experiment, to make*
> *mistakes without me looking over her shoulder. The freedom to*
> *express herself, to talk the way she wants to the animals. The*
> *freedom to leave the phone unanswered when I call.*

I felt trapped in the *Can't Zone*. By observing my state, however, I turned my C-Zone emotional state into the *Change Zone* that leads to the *Being Zone*, the reflective zone. I was honest about my feelings and did not try to suppress, deny or justify them. As I reflected, I held fast to the principles and the faith by which I choose to govern my life. Through the power of my will—through choice—I resisted the negative feelings. In the next paragraph, I weighed the consequences of divorce more realistically:

And I. What would I gain? The freedom to drive myself further into despair? The opportunity to work harder for less? The disapproval of my children and alienation from my friends? A little control maybe, but mostly it would be death. Maybe another woman would come along who might be all that Cathy isn't, but most certainly she wouldn't be all that Cathy is. Then I would see what I've been blind to these past twenty years. And I'd miss her.

So how can I give her what she needs now? And how can I find the motivation to do this? How can I stop looking over her shoulder and avoid criticizing her? How can I be more appreciative of all that she is, all that she is doing for the family and me.

How can I?

By acknowledging my negative thoughts and feelings and by giving myself permission to feel them and explore them in the safety of my journal, they began to dissipate. This entry was not pleasant to write, and it is embarrassing to share. Even a strong marriage, however, goes through rough spots, and everyone who lives in zones A or B most of the time will experience C-Zone failures periodically.

My aim in life is to spend as little time in the C-Zone as possible. Before I can escape the C-Zone, though, I must recognize that I have slipped into it. I must admit the fear, the shame, the anxiety, the perfectionism, the pride, and even the underlying anger that are the warning signs of C-Zone life.

THE EMOTIONAL GYM

When I suggest that you acknowledge your feelings and past failures, I am not suggesting that you go on a massive search-and-destroy mission, in which you unearth every nook and cranny of your past. In fact, you may have done too much of that already. It is a characteristic to engage in unhealthy introspection and navel-gazing while in the C-Zone. The victim mentality feeds into blaming your parents or a sibling, blaming the materialistic culture, the school system or anything else for making you what you are.

Now that you are familiar with all of the Zones, it is time to start working out. The emotional gym—the workout room—is the *Being Zone*, the place for productive reflection as opposed to unproductive navel-gazing and harmful introspection. The exercises in the *Workout* section of this book will show you how to engage in healthy reflection so that you can emerge from your quiet time more emotionally fit.

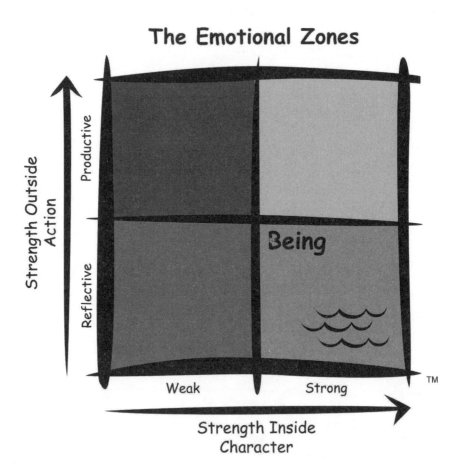

CHAPTER FIVE 5:

THE BEING ZONE

THE AGONY OF WAITING

W hat happens when you reach a railroad crossing just as a long, slow train is passing? Would you rather drive an extra mile to beat the train to another crossing, knowing that you will lose time and money on extra gas and wear and tear on the vehicle?

I would.

If you are like me, you feel better moving. You do not like to be held up by a train, a traffic jam, or a meeting that is going nowhere. When I know where I want to go, I want to push through. "Get outta my way!" I mutter under my breath. Resting, listening, pondering a better way, sitting in centered silence, relaxing my breath and my mind or meditating on a meaningful passage from an uplifting book are difficult for me. For men of action, the resting, reflection, and waiting inherent to the *Being Zone* are uncomfortable. Sitting still is hard work. In fact, this place of rest does not feel at all restful. The *Being Zone* is supposed to be a quiet and comfortable place, yet when we stop there, we find ourselves filled with turmoil.

The *Being Zone* feels like a place of tension. There, we become aware of the turmoil and negative emotions that our busyness prevents us from seeing. We face a conundrum. We enter the *Being Zone* and want to do something—anything—to release the building tension. However, we must resist that desire and practice becoming still—the work of waiting.

Despite the perils, all men should choose to enter the *Being Zone* on a regular basis for reflection and renewal. It is our emotional workout space.

An emotionally healthy man makes regular, planned trips to the *Being Zone*, where he reflects on any mistakes and weaknesses, identifying and disclosing them. He sees what needs to be changed, finds the root causes, resolves to change, then goes back into the *Actualizing Zone* where he practices what he has learned.

You can maintain your A-Zone inner and outer strength only through anchoring yourself in the times of B-Zone reflection. It may be the hardest work you will ever do, but the results are dramatic if you make B-Zone time a habit.

The Emotional Zones

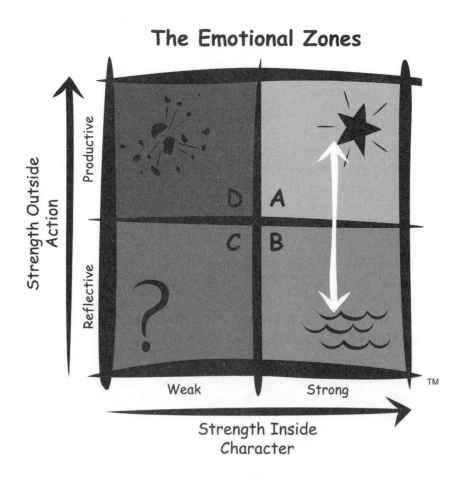

PLAN TO REST

When following a planned physical fitness program, rest times between workouts are essential, because they allow your body to recover. If you do not have enough rest, you can overstress your body and injure yourself. In the emotional arena, if you do not learn to take the necessary rest time, you are creating a sure recipe for burnout and explosive behavior.

When planning an emotional training program, it is important to have regular rest times. That means locking your rest times into your schedule. If you do not write your B-Zone time on your calendar, you will become so busy you will easily push through your rest times.

Why do we find rest and reflection so difficult? Partially because our identity is so tied up in what we do. If we are not busy doing, we feel below par, insecure, and less of a man. How ridiculous! Athletes do not doubt they are athletes when they are off the field or off the court.

Being is a vital precursor to *doing*. When we focus on our state of being, we can understand better who we are, clarify our purpose, and become fit for our game. Then we can compete in the challenges we face. Our doing takes on a new dimension. It spreads goodwill. It helps rather than harms. It gets us out of emotional sand traps with one graceful stroke.

Too often, we men are geared toward competition. Times of quiet reflection—intense questioning regarding our motives and our purpose; waiting, listening, waiting, pondering, and waiting some more for the right answer to show up; being content with silence, with simplicity, with the peace of inactivity—are too difficult for us. So we skip our workouts in the *Being Zone* and become emotionally flabby and weak. Then our character begins to break down.

Being is a vital precursor to doing.

We must discipline ourselves to take these moments, to relish these times, and schedule them as necessary appointments in our daily routine. Scheduling them in the morning is the most effective, because there is less chance of interruption. It is too easy to get busy, so we need to stay away from e-mail, voice mail and any work-related items and focus solely on being still.

Doing so allows answers we need during the day to show up when we are not seeking them consciously. Even if we do not think we need them, these answers can pop into our minds and solve problems we may not have been contemplating. What a wonderful way to increase productivity!

RIGHT REFLECTION

The *Being Zone* is the check-up zone. It is our daily fitness test. It is where we look for emotional injuries or challenges we need to address. Discouragement, despondency, frustration, confusion, anger, blame, resentment, worry, and anxiety indicate the need for more time in the B-Zone. It is a lot easier to enter the *Being Zone* as a preventive measure than to go there after we are upset.

Because our conscience is specific about wrongful behavior that needs to change, we do not have to go on search-and-destroy missions to unearth the secrets of our past, armed with the latest self-help book. In fact, it is often pride that makes us want to barge into the dark corners and hidden closets of our souls. It is like trying to clean up the house before the professional cleaning crew gets there. We do not want anyone to see what slobs we have been. It is the same with our emotional health. We figure that if we get in there before we let someone else know our thoughts, we can perfect ourselves.

Sorry, but it does not work that way. Self-illumination will never supply enough light to do the job. There is, however, a Light of Truth that does not come from us, a Light with a capital "L" that reveals our inner selves if we will stand still long enough for it to expose what needs healing. We can rest and allow this Light to shine into those secret closets that are full of skeletons. With the help of our conscience, this Light will make us aware of the specific things we need to change. No massive guilt trip, just resting and allowing the Light of Truth to dissolve our anger, our fear, our anxiety, and our worry and to reveal the steps necessary to make things right.

When you enter the *Being Zone*, resist the temptation to wallow in your past. You might be telling yourself something like, "At age three, my father beat up my mother in front of me, and that explains the way I am today." Your focus on past trauma may lead you to believe that change is impossible. Instead of fixating on the past, allow yourself to observe these thoughts, but do not dwell on them or believe them.

The more you contemplate the character and behavior you choose to express, the sooner you will start to behave that way.

Focus on the future. Think about the person that you want to be. Imagine yourself as someone who is emotionally strong and loving, with a resilient, consistent character. The more you contemplate the character and behavior you choose to express, the sooner you will start to behave that way. Focus on creating what you want instead of what you do not want. Images about yourself that you hold in your mind have a powerful effect in shaping future behavior. That is why you want to see your future self in a positive light rather than constantly throwing up negative pictures from previous experiences.

FORCED REST

In addition to your planned "rest times" in the *Being Zone*, you can learn to take advantage of reflective times such as waiting at the doctor's office or commuting long distances. You can enter the B-Zone while you wait or drive, instead of reading a magazine or listening to the radio.

In football, the players warm up on their own first, then with the team. The coach then psyches them up with a pep talk in the locker room. Finally, it is time to hit the field. The players run through the tunnel and are greeted by cheering fans.

The players are ready to go, but the game has not begun. They have to stand still for the national anthem. They face a time of forced rest. It is a tough time for players who are pumped and ready to go. Those who stay relaxed while focusing on the impending game get into the flow at kick-off. The players are also forced to rest at half-time, which is equivalent to a third of the game in length.

In his book *Halftime*, Bob Buford uses this period as a metaphor for the time of forced rest and reflection men face at mid-life. He describes how difficult it is for men to give themselves permission to be there. "We find greater satisfaction from the thrill of the chase than from the successful completion of the conquest," Buford writes. "Burying ourselves in the hustle and bustle of daily existence, we rarely take time out to experience the wonder and stillness of solitude, where the quiet voice of God is most audible."[1]

Sometimes, the greatest strengths of a B-Zone man can also become drawbacks.

Look at your times of forced rest as similar to what football players face during the national anthem or at half-time. Choose to appreciate this state rather than fight it. Use it to reflect rather than escape. The mid-life crises men face are so predictable, they resemble a rite of passage. We may also face other times of forced rest when tragedy strikes, such as illness, divorce or death of a loved one. You may be reading this book because you have faced a tragedy of some sort. Often, we do not know why bad things happen and innocent people suffer. Sometimes, tragedies are the consequences of our choices and behavior patterns.

Maybe someone you love gave you this book and told you to shape up—or else! You may be in a position where you are forced to reflect on your life, because if you do not take time out and find a way to change, catastrophe awaits. Maybe the catastrophe has already happened, and you are responsible for creating it. Either way, it is never too late to turn your life around. But it is far better to go to the *Being Zone* as a preventive measure than a corrective one. If you make it a regular practice, you can avoid the blow-ups that come as a consequence of your anger or inability to connect with your loved ones. You will also be better prepared for the trials and tragedies that life brings whether you are at fault or not.

MAKING A DIFFERENCE

Some people stay static in the *Being Zone*, always reflecting on their character and "working on it" but never testing it or trying to make an impact on the world around them. As men, we have a creative responsibility to make a difference in the world. A man who lives in the B-Zone most of the time has got to step into the A-Zone to get things done, to see results.

Sometimes the greatest strengths of a B-Zone man can also become drawbacks. For example, the B-Zone ability to experience empathy can be a great communication tool and make others around us feel wonderful, but when circumstances demand effectiveness, empathy is risky. Whether it is disciplining a child we love or an employee who fails to meet the targets, we need to learn how to keep empathy from sabotaging the very effectiveness required to lovingly correct or help people. Sometimes, moving forward means that someone we love will experience short-term pain.

A friend of mine, I'll call him Cameron, is a man who believes in "live and let live." He describes himself as an artistic nurturer. He would rate high in all the positive, reflective traits that characterize the B-Zone. He says it is not in his nature to push for results. Thus, he does not enter the A-Zone as much as he could or should.

In thinking about Cameron's desire to avoid hurting people, I realized he is concerned about the D-Zone's gravitational pull. It appears to me that Cameron sees the productive side of my graph as one quadrant instead of two. He views all productive people as being in the *Destructive Zone*, a place where relationships become casualties, as opposed to the *Actualizing Zone*, a place where relationships are enhanced and legacies are created.

When a B-Zone man equates productivity with destructiveness, it explains his reluctance to venture into the productive *Actualizing Zone*. Because relationships are paramount, he is concerned that others will misunderstand him if he takes action. But if we are emotionally fit, we can find ways to stand up for ourselves, keep a team on track, show leadership, and discipline people under our authority in a way that also communicates our deep concern for them. By remaining static in the *Being Zone*, men risk compromising their principles, though they might not see it this way. However, as the great political philosopher Edmund Burke once said, "All that is needed for the forces of evil to triumph is for good men to do nothing."

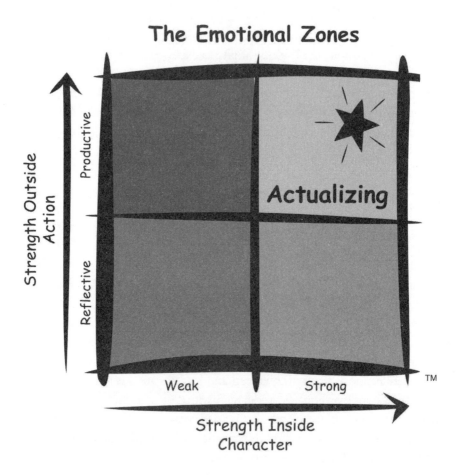

CHAPTER 6:

THE ACTUALIZING ZONE

ROLE MODELS

Professional athletes are some of the highest-profile role models for a young boy. Sadly, the private lives of many do not parallel their performances on the field, court or rink. But what happens when an athlete turns out to be as great a guy off the playing field as he is during the game? We take notice. If the star golfer or tennis player is a faithful family man and a selfless worker on behalf of the underprivileged, he is held up as the real deal. Even the way a star gives an autograph tells us something about him.

"I got Tiger Wood's autograph, and he was really nice!" we might say, as if it surprises us that a larger-than-life superstar would stoop to be kind. It is awesome when an athlete combines performance with a strong inner character.

That is the alignment we want to achieve in our emotional workout. Men in the *Actualizing Zone* are strong inside and outside. They are productive and effective as well as men of high character and emotional strength. They are authentic.

Maybe you have spent time in the A-Zone already, and you enjoy the way it feels. Perhaps you are not sure how you found yourself in the *Actualizing Zone*—a place where you have effortlessly said the right thing at the right time. Your actions were unselfish, loving, and wise, leaving you with a clear conscience. Your actions had a positive effect on everyone around you. You want more of the A-Zone, but you are not sure how you managed to sink what felt like a hole-in-one. You may be asking, "Was it just a fluke?" Let's examine some specific qualities of a man in the *Actualizing Zone* so you will know exactly what you are aiming for.

LEADERSHIP QUALITIES

In leadership training circles, it is common to gather around a flip chart or a white board while a facilitator leads a brainstorming session on the qualities of a leader. Interestingly, almost every group will come up with a list of characteristics similar to those that follow:

- Has vision
- Has integrity
- Communicates effectively
- Listens intently
- Inspires, encourages, and motivates others
- Takes charge
- Knows what he is doing; has the right expertise
- Is willing to defer to the expertise of others
- Is unafraid to have people on staff who are smarter than him or her
- Can be a team player and allow others to lead when necessary
- Commands respect
- Cares about people
- Gets the job done
- Learns continually
- Allows others to voice their thoughts; seeks input
- Empowers others; allows the creativity of others to shine
- Gives credit to others when due. Does not hog the limelight
- Is accountable

- Is willing to admit faults and take steps to correct them
- Doesn't expect perfection of others, and corrects mistakes appropriately
- Is passionate
- Keeps a promise
- Knows how to delegate

You can add your own thoughts to this list. Most of these leadership qualities are character traits that are not related to any single personality type. Good leadership does not depend on whether you are an introvert or an extrovert. Anyone can get to the A-Zone if they develop the right character traits and learn the appropriate leadership skills.

CHARACTER AT WORK

At work, a leader in the *Actualizing Zone* takes responsibility. As US President Harry Truman used to say, "The buck stops here." That means an A-Zone man holds himself and others accountable for their actions. He keeps things on time and on line. He is more than a manager though, because he has vision—he knows where he wants the team to go. He values the input and insight of others and his ability to communicate allows them to buy into his vision. He inspires and encourages them to contribute their creativity toward realizing the team's goals.

An A-Zone man lives by sound moral principles that guide him even when no one is looking. He is not going to cook the books just because he can get away with it. In this era of Enron-type accounting scandals, where even professional accountants have made numbers say what they want them to say, there is an ever-greater need for character. A-Zone men stand up for what is right and wholesome in their workplaces. They lead by example and set a positive tone for others to follow.

TEAMWORK

The quarterback of a football team is not supposed to bash through the opposition's defensive line. He has the big boys around him to

> *An A-Zone man lives by sound moral principles that guide him even when no one is looking.*

do that. Similarly, in the workplace, an A-Zone leader knows he needs a team of people around him to compensate for areas where he is not as strong or as interested. He also needs people to whom he can delegate so that his valuable time is used to best advantage. For example, if you are someone who always sees the bright side, you need a person on your team with insight into potential problems. If you hate to worry about details, make sure at least one team member is a "facts and figures" person.

A-Zone men know how to delegate. They communicate clear expectations and then empower others to make the necessary decisions that will lead to success. D-Zone men may be brilliant and creative, but they lack the skills to get everyone on the same page without using intimidation. They may feel that no one can do a task as well as they can, so they breathe over their subordinates' shoulders. In contrast, A-Zone men inspire respect, not fear. Instead of being control freaks, they know how to guide, encourage, and mentor those around them. They take the time to develop their team members.

These men are not afraid to have people on their team outshine them. They have confidence in their own abilities and are comfortable enough with themselves to appreciate when the spotlight shines on someone else. They enjoy giving credit to others. They spend time building bridges, soliciting feedback, and being pro-active so problems do not grow out of proportion. The lowliest team member does not fear giving an A-Zone leader bad news, because that leader is willing to act on problems while they are still small enough to contain or eliminate. An A-Zone man understands his emotions and does not vent his anger. He responds to problems appropriately. This builds trust amongst his team members. He wants people to tell him freely they have made a mistake, knowing that he will reply with wisdom and thoughtfulness.

When you operate in the *Actualizing Zone*, you understand that people are not the problem. Most often, the opponent is injustice, poor strategy or self-defeating behaviors. You see the blocks *in* people, the hindrances that make them less effective. You focus on the problem rather than the person and are careful not to hurt them. Instead, you help people overcome internal blockages, listen carefully to real objectives, and create solutions that allow everyone to win.

Arriving at win/win solutions is not easy. Many view this as compromising—an ugly word to most men. But an A-Zone leader may deem achieving a consensus as the most effective course of action. It is a calculated decision that requires patience and vision. Reaching consensus in the A-Zone is far different than achieving consensus in the C-Zone. In the *Can't Zone*, it means giving way without considering one's own needs. It is capitulating to force or bowing under pressure. Even if a C-Zone man knows what is right, he experiences confusion. Doubting himself and his abilities, he lacks the backbone and strength to make sure his position is communicated and argued effectively. Instead, he folds, and his emotional weakness masquerades as consensus-building behavior. He ends up with a win/lose scenario, and he's on the losing end.

In the *Actualizing Zone*, consensus results from a tremendous effort to understand. It involves listening actively and sizing up the challenges and opportunities effectively. It demands discernment and solid, strategic thinking.

When facing critical challenges, those in the A-Zone prepare by entering into deep reflection in the *Being Zone*. There, these men assess their abilities and character to accomplish the task at hand without hurting others. They care about everyone's well being, even when their decisions look harsh. The A-Zone man's effect on a team

A-Zone men inspire respect, not fear. Instead of being control freaks, they know how to guide, encourage, and mentor those around them.

When facing critical challenges, those in the A-Zone prepare by entering deep into reflection in the Being Zone.

looks like magic, when in fact it is based on solid principles and character that anyone can build if they commit the necessary time and effort.

How often do we see leaders in the workplace exhibit A-Zone character traits? Not often enough. Unfortunately, we usually see D-Zone men running the show. When a D-Zone man is in control, someone loses out. Less frequently, we see C-Zone men in positions of power. When that happens, the C-Zone man may have the title and the salary but he is unable to run anything, and chaos results.

CHARACTER AT HOME

Just as no sports team can succeed without a coach, all the members of a team cannot be coaches at the same time. As a man, your role in the family is that of coach or leader. You are the one who is supposed to be the final authority, the "buck stops here" husband and father. But that does not mean you treat your wife and kids like servants. In the family, the A-Zone man represents good and proper authority

While some men abdicate their leadership role and leave it to their wives, other men abuse their authority by lording it over everyone. It is D-Zone to act like a dictator in your home and demand that others serve you as if they were cleaning staff. It is C-Zone to sit back and let your wife run the show.

It is A-Zone to pull your own weight, A-Zone to share in menial tasks that go into running a household, and A-Zone to train your children to help with household chores, patiently building character traits of discipline and responsibility into them. An A-Zone father gets a team approach going so that work gets done and no one person ends up alone on the drudge detail.

An A-Zone man is responsible *for* himself and *to* his wife and kids. As a leader, he serves his family and leads by example. His authority is not a power trip; it springs from within, from strong character and sound principles. An A-Zone man practices servant leadership. He considers the needs of his family above his own. He is willing to go the extra mile to make sure he looks after their material needs as well as their emotional and spiritual needs.

> *Try looking after the needs of others, and you will find that your own needs are met in ways you could never imagine.*

An A-Zone man lives by principles rather than letting his feelings guide him. He knows that feelings fluctuate, and sometimes he has to bring his feelings into line with his principled actions rather than vice versa. He might not feel like listening to his wife or reading a story to his child; he would rather read the sports page or watch the news. But he chooses to do what is loving and unselfish for the good of his wife or child.

All of this may seem impossible to you. You may think that putting others first will feel like dying. If so, ask yourself the following questions: Do you usually put your needs first? If so, how happy are you? Try looking after the needs of others, and you will find that your own needs are met in ways you could never imagine. You will find happiness and deep satisfaction awaiting you in the *Actualizing Zone.*

RESULTS MATTER

Not having the proper skills affects your ability to act. So, if you are weak on skills like communication, time management or goal setting, you may not have the results you want at work or in your family no matter how principled you are. However, as an A-Zone man, you can acknowledge your weaknesses, and your strength of character leads you to find ways to improve.

SWEATING FROM YOUR EYES

In the *Actualizing Zone,* you are a life-long learner and are always adding new skills to your game. You are aware of how your actions—both good and bad—affect those around you. Your workout program is designed to develop your character and skills so that you can overcome harmful actions. Living in the *Actualizing Zone,* you will have the ability to be and act.

In my years of corporate training, I have met many individuals who talk eloquently about principles, values, and ethics but rarely teach how to find them and live by them. Instead, they move on quickly to teach leadership skills. The trainers seem to send a message that once someone learns these skills, he or she becomes a better person automatically.

Sometimes we buy into this message. We think, "I've learned the skill, therefore I'm a better listener and communicator." However, learning and practicing a skill for a while may change our outward appearance, but it does not change our character. Remember my high school acting story? Yes, smiling more and changing your body language to reflect a listening posture will often change the outcome of your interactions with others, because they will often respond with a smile and a willingness to open up. However, if the intent of your new smile is to ensure that you get your own way, then it becomes a form of manipulation, not emotional fitness.

That is why you see many successful men who shine on the surface. They look like A-Zone men, because they have all the skills down pat. But inside, they are still in the D-Zone. They might have great charisma and communication skills. They can dazzle and fool us with their sleight of hand. But learning the skills without building the right kind of character is a way of conning yourself and others. An A-Zone man is clear on his purpose and his principles. His conscience is clear when it comes to how he relates to others. If a smile is genuine and spontaneous, then it is a true expression without any manipulative strings attached. Though this may be a simple example, I am sure it resonates with you.

We all have had days when we had to paste on a face to get something done. If you are at all sensitive, you feel compromised while doing so; your feelings and expressions are disconnected. Those in the A-Zone want to make their inner and outer states congruent. They want to be genuine. To attain and maintain this sense of alignment with the inner and the outer world, they spend a great deal of time in the *Being Zone*.

Learning the skills without building the right kind of character is a way of conning yourself and others.

A-Zone men manage their emotions well, because they are in tune with their feelings at any given moment and can sense their impact on others. They are like a good sailor who understands how to capture the wind and fine-tune the sails so the boat moves where he wants it to go. In the same way, an A-Zone man knows how to govern his emotions and act on principle instead of letting negative feelings buffet him around. Individuals in the A-Zone can motivate themselves and others toward greatness. They stand up for causes and break new ground where others fear to tread.

In conclusion, let us look at one of our favorite sports scenarios: Against all odds, an underdog team rises above its circumstances, rallies together, and overcomes more skillful opponents. The team's energy, zeal, and determination are things we all admire and long for. That is what is possible in the A-Zone. No matter how much of an underdog you may feel like right now, you can learn to live and win in the A-Zone. The difference it will make in your life and the lives of those around you will be dramatic and rewarding.

PART II:
THE WORKOUT

The Emotional Zones

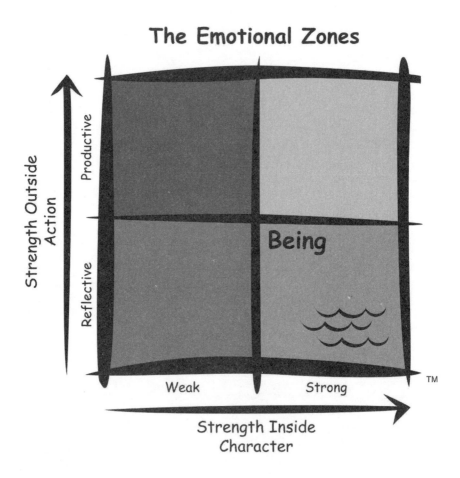

START RIGHT

By now, you have filled out your survey and have plotted the survey results from others. You now know what Zone you are in most of the time and the ones you have a tendency to slip into if you are not careful. You know your "emotional fat index" and your Target Zone "heart rate." Now it is time to start working out.

The remaining chapters offer a range of exercises to help you build emotional fitness. Do not let the sheer number of exercises or suggested techniques overwhelm you. You do not have to do them all. However, if you do one or two of these exercises faithfully every day, you will see a big improvement in your inner strength. The key is to make these exercises a habit. As physical fitness experts say, you need to make fitness and a proper diet part of your lifestyle. I am asking you to do the same thing with your emotional fitness. Start small, pace yourself; add an exercise and a technique or two at a time. After a few weeks of practice, your newly developed habits will prepare you for even greater challenges.

While researching this book, I ran into some of the same problems you are likely to face when you begin a new self-help program. Seeking to explore the parallels between emotional and physical fitness, I decided to try out a new gym and found a friend to go with me. (Finding workout buddies is one of the key emotional workout principles in this book.) My friend Bruce knew the gym's owner and had worked out

Start small, pace yourself; add an exercise and a technique or two at a time.

a good deal for us. The club had great equipment and is not overly busy. On our first day, we decided to try one of the free spin classes using stationary bikes.

We showed up late and had trouble finding the change room. When we joined the class, the warm-up had already begun. The participants had met ten times and were already in shape. I couldn't keep up. It stretched me just to finish the workout.

Spinning is about endurance, expanding your cardiovascular capacity. But that morning, I could barely keep my legs going. During the workout, we were told to spin as fast as possible to get our heart rates up to ninety percent of maximum. I only pushed myself to spin a little faster, knowing that if I hammered it, I would not last the full forty-five minutes.

Afterwards, Bruce and I wandered around the gym. I had never seen most of the equipment before. The exercise machines were ergonomically safe, but I did not know how to use them. Where do I sit? What muscles would they work? How much weight could I put on?

Bruce was more comfortable than I was. He wandered around, sat, lay down or stood inside various machines. He experimented with weight and had a good feel for the place. He was still grazing, but I had had enough. Uncomfortable with being out of my element, I wanted to clean up and get out of there.

You might feel the same way when you first start your emotional workouts. You will be tempted to compare your performance against others. If they seem more relaxed, comfortable or fit, you may be tempted to drop out. No one likes to see himself in a bad light compared to others. However, you may discover the guys who appear comfortable are just as nervous as you are.

When I returned home from the gym, I asked myself a number of questions. If I go back with Bruce, will he help motivate me? Will his workout style match mine? Do I want to help him meet his goals or do I only care about myself? I needed to clarify my goals, my time, the amount of energy required, and the sacrifices necessary to sustain my efforts.

After reviewing the day, I decided I had made a false start on my physical fitness program. You may discover the same thing. The guys you thought would make great emotional workout buddies are not interested in going in the same direction as you. You find that your initial discomfort with the "equipment" or the "workout space" does not go away. Do not use this discomfort as an excuse to stop working out. Instead, adjust your course of action. You may need to use a different approach or find another group, workout partner or "gym." It is important to understand that you are in the wrong place at the right time. This may mean making the difficult decision to move on. Do not settle for less than you know is possible. And do not let setbacks make you quit.

Keep experimenting until you find the right combination of workout routines.

Some of the exercises in this book may not work for you. Keep experimenting until you find the right combination of workout routines. You will also be tempted to seek the easy way out. That is why choosing a workout buddy you trust can make a huge difference to your success. We all need a "spotter," and we can benefit by "spotting" for someone else. We can also encourage each other to work harder than we might if we were on our own.

CHAPTER 7:

WORKOUT BUDDIES

GROWING TOGETHER

As boys, we liked to experiment, to roughhouse, and learn from each other. We missed balls on the playing field and celebrated the ones we caught. We fell out of trees, got tangled up in our bicycles, scraped knees, and broke bones. We challenged and chided each other and learned not only by doing but also by competing alongside and against our friends. We worked out with our buddies and developed our skills that way.

As adults, we still need a peer group that will challenge us on an emotional level. We need guys to push us, buddies to help us up when we fall; friends to run beside us during the emotional marathon of life. By meeting regularly, we can help each other compete and win in life, where what's at stake is not just pride, a bag of licorice or baseball cards, but the future of our marriages, the success of our children, and the well being of our families and communities.

> *We need guys to push us, buddies to help us up when we fall; friends to run beside us during the emotional marathon of life.*

ABANDONING THE GAME

If a pro showed up at a baseball field full of kids and said, "Hey, you guys mind if I hit a few?" the wide-eyed boys would drop their gloves and move off to the side. I believe that most of us behave the same way with our wives. We defer to them, because they are better than we are at handling emotions and emotional confrontations. When feelings run high at home, our wives step in and we retreat to the sidelines to let the "experts" handle things. Or, if we do step in, we resort to pushing our weight around, as if might makes right.

One reason most men either demand their way or avoid emotional confrontation altogether is that we are emotionally weak. We are responding according to the fight-or-flight syndrome. A man may appear to be winning because he has a big house and lots of toys, but his emotional track record is littered with relational casualties that would leave any pro team at the bottom of the standings. As boys, we learned how to win at the physical game. But when it came to the inner emotional game, we did not even show up for practice.

Many men believe a relationship with their wife or girlfriend is all they need for their emotional workout. They do not have any close male friends. I believe these men do not know they are wrestling out of their weight class. Women are not supposed to be our emotional sparring partners. We are not even playing in the same league as they are! We fool ourselves by thinking they are weak, because every month hormonal changes accost them, which often coincides with our continual expectations or criticisms wearing them down. Too often, we take them for granted.

Men need other men. We have tried far too long to be on the same emotional playing field as our wives.

Men need other men. We have tried far too long to be on the same emotional playing field as our wives. We end up in a brawl with heavyweights and get our butts kicked. Worse yet, we spar with our children and do immeasurable damage. Every time we blow our tops, remain isolated or emotionally disconnected, we lose. We are living in an emotional danger zone. We do not know how to relate effectively or positively in the emotional arena. We have to learn how to play the emotional game. The new rules may be intimidating, but if we do not learn to play by them, we will not go far. As kids, we hated those who did not play by the rules, and, as men, that reality has not changed.

What our wives need are strong men who can stand up to life's pressures yet be kind enough to put their own agendas aside for their wives' sake. We need to handle a crisis at the end of a long day with patience and wisdom if we hope to build the kind of trust and safety that promotes freedom and growth in our children and emotional security in our spouses. This is where our workout buddies can help.

We cannot win at the game of life if we do not work out emotionally. We need to practice the necessary skills on a daily basis. And whether we are in the major leagues or just starting out, practicing with our workout buddies prepares us for the real deal.

You are already in the game, so why not exercise with your teammates, your workout partners? Get out on the emotional "field" with other men and discuss the winning plays. Join a team of men who encourage each other, whether they hit a home run or strike out three times in a row. Just as we committed ourselves to our buddies as kids, commit yourself to work out with other men who want to improve their emotional abilities, men who will listen and offer counsel, men who are dependable week after week. Working out with your buddies can be a wild adventure. I compare it to the exhilaration of mountain biking with a bunch of guys who push you to your limit. The smell of the forest, the speed, the rides at night with the lights on all intensify the enjoyment and the adrenaline rush. This is how euphoric your emotional workouts with other men can be.

Some boys never experience the joy of sports. They never sign up, because the skills do not come easily or they stomp away when someone makes fun of them. It is the same with our emotions. Many men were never invited to share their feelings early in life, and those who tried were told to "Butt out! You're acting like a girl. Be a man!" Now they

When you work out with a bunch of guys, you challenge each other to stretch, to take risks, to compete in healthy ways and develop new skills.

are afraid of the challenges and miss out on the invigoration of being in shape emotionally.

Anyone who participates in sports knows the joy of being *in* the game. When you work out with a bunch of guys, you challenge each other to stretch, to take risks, to compete in healthy ways and develop new skills. My fitness trainer, Chris Munford, is a former professional football player. Apart from the game itself, what he misses most since retiring is being with the other players. Those of us who work out to become emotionally fit also know the exhilaration of sharing the process of inner transformation with others. We share the joy of adventure that comes with uncertainty and challenges.

There are two ways to stay away from the emotional game: 1) you can opt out and avoid growth or 2) you can also stay in the game in a haphazard way but not push yourself, treading water to maintain a status quo. Do not assume that because you have male friends with whom you play cards or meet with for coffee that you have workout buddies. Most interactions between men remain highly superficial.

MENSPEAK

Not everyone makes a good companion on the road to emotional fitness. Men interact with each other all the time, but not on the level I am talking about. In fact, a lot of male bonding is shallow. It often focuses on trivial things as a way to avoid facing emotional brokenness and failure.

I like to spend time alone on my motorcycle. One afternoon, while giving my seat a rest and warming my hands around a steaming mug of coffee at a donut shop, I sat beside two guys in their mid-forties. Wearing baseball hats and jackets emblazoned with sports logos, they seemed like old friends, comfortable with each other and their surroundings. I've often been a part of the guy talk that followed, but this time I decided to take out my pen and write down the gist of their conversation.

"Good game?" The larger one asked. "How many people were there?"

"About six thousand," the smaller man said. "They had to bring in extra seats to take the extra crowds. They missed some real opportunities to make money. I would have bought a hat had they had some for sale. I guess the only guy that is aware enough to make those decisions is too busy. Lost the game though, they did."

"Oh?"

"Yeah. When it comes right down to it, you have to do both: have a great offence and a great defense. They really lost the game in the second half."

The men ate their donuts and sipped their coffee. Then, after a long pause, more talk.

"Remember Sam?" The smaller man asked. "He's got two sons playing there. One's a defensive guard and the other's a quarterback. His eldest son came into the game in the second quarter. He really sparked them when he came in. He got a lot of time on the field this year."

"That so?"

"Yeah, well, Sam's kid got all the way to the one-yard line, and then some first-year rookie stopped him dead in his tracks. Surprised the hell out of him. Missed his chance to score and turn it around when it really mattered."

We are all familiar with conversations like these. Guy talk. "Menspeak." About sports. About toys. About strategy. About winners and losers. About things. About stuff. Big talk that puffs us up. Who's making money and who's not? Who's on top today? Comparative talk. "Mine has a 427 with a supercharger and a four-barrel. What's yours got?"

Mine's faster. Mine's more expensive. If mine isn't bigger, at least I can use it better. We're all trophy hunters of some sort, and if we cannot buy them, we dream that some day we will. We think our trophies will take all our problems away.

"Check that out." "Whew, did you see her?" Compare. Evaluate. "Am I on top?" "Do I rate?"

This constant verbal competition shuts out the real issues. We stay at the surface, ignoring the scars from previous wounds. We keep a safe distance from all that makes us vulnerable, doing our best to come off as though we are okay. If we cannot be on top, we talk about those who are, and we gloat when they fall because it helps us feel better about our own failures. Our inability to talk about what really matters causes us to miss out on big opportunities to change the outcome of the game we are in.

Our inability to talk about what really matters causes us to miss out on big opportunities to change the outcome of the game we are in.

When I met with Paul Henderson, I told him about that overheard conversation in the donut shop. I wondered if men like that will ever develop a hunger for truth. I asked Paul what he would say to guys like that. "Some of them aren't even aware of the problem," he said. "They have operated at that level for so long they are comfortable." Is a fear of revealing weakness behind all the "mine is bigger than yours" talk we hear among men? I think so, and so does Paul. "If you keep things on a superficial level you do not have to show you are weak. Most guys aren't even aware that there is another level," he says.

That is sad, but I believe it is also true. Most guys do not know what they are missing by hiding behind small talk that masquerades as big talk.

REVEAL WHO YOU ARE

One of the most difficult emotional exercises you will ever do, either by yourself or with other men, is to reveal your weaknesses. Some of us are so busy running away from ourselves that we might not even be aware we have any. But we all do, and what a life-changing experience it can be to finally confess them to others and ourselves.

Once you become vulnerable with like-minded men, you will find that something new kicks in and the real you will come to life. You will feel the same sense of elation you felt when you ran bases on the field in your first ball game. As you acknowledge your weaknesses, you will become more authentic. By zeroing in on the areas you need to change, you will find yourself improving in the emotional arena even if the pain and awareness of your flaws seems overwhelming.

The pain is temporary. Think of it as sore muscles needing an ice pack after your first time in the weight room. Soon, the pain will pass. Your muscles will grow stronger, and you will be lifting bigger weights and gaining emotional definition in no time.

When we discover our real selves emerging from beneath our camouflage, we become bigger, better, stronger men. And we find out that others share the same weaknesses and fears as we do.

CHOOSE CAREFULLY

Choose your workout buddies carefully. You do not want to disclose personal matters to people who are going to gossip about you, lord it over you or ridicule you. One of the traits of men stuck in the *Can't Zone* is inappropriate disclosure. They tell the wrong people the wrong information at the wrong time. They get burned, and such experiences become an excuse to remain passive. Find a safe place and safe people with whom to share your deepest concerns and weaknesses. Make sure your workout buddies respect confidentiality.

If you start your own men's group, it is important that you show vulnerability first. Make sure you do not use sarcasm against other members of the group or put people

Make sure your workout buddies respect confidentiality.

105

down. Before joining an established group, look for vulnerability in the leader.

My life's passion is to connect with men, knowing intuitively that my emotional and spiritual survival depends on developing the right kind of friends and having the right kind of mentors. I remember the first time I had lunch with a man who struck me as someone I wanted to get to know. I asked him if he would consider becoming friends. My words were like a leap of faith, and I trusted we would connect. I have done this with others as well. Trust is about risking vulnerability.

Your workout buddies need to be honest, even if what they tell you is not pleasant to hear. They can help you to see yourself objectively, bringing your weaknesses to light. That is when the workouts can get tough, but the benefits are priceless.

Paul Henderson told me he makes time to receive input from others. Their words have made him realize that he needs more patience, gentleness, and humility. He has told his wife and some close friends that he wants to be held accountable for improving in these areas. He discloses his weaknesses willingly and makes himself answerable to these selected people.

> *A commitment to change and mutual accountability will empower right action and right behavior and build emotional strength and character for all group members.*

Have you chosen to be accountable to anyone in your life? Have people close to you been trying to tell you how you come across for a long time? If so, perhaps it is time for you to *own* your weaknesses—take responsibility for them—and listen to what these people have to say.

Paul says he asks himself constantly, "Have I done anything to hurt someone?" This makes him aware of the times he is in the *Destructive Zone*. He drops his "strong on the outside" pose, reveals his weaknesses, and apologizes. That is an example of going from the C-Zone into the B-Zone to find forgiveness, healing, and accountability.

You can do the same thing with your workout buddies. If you are working out properly, all of you will reveal traits or weaknesses from the *Destructive* and *Can't Zones*. You will identify those gaps between who you would like to be and who you really are. You will strengthen each other through mutual encouragement, honest advice, concerned council, and effective prayer. A commitment to change and mutual accountability will empower right action and right behavior and build emotional strength and character for all group members.

During your meetings, make sure no one engages in derogatory behavior or gossip about people outside the group. A quick way to destroy trust is to put other people down when they are not around.

PROTECTIVE GEAR

Whether you are a sports nut, an occasional player or someone who watches from the sidelines, you know that specific sports-related gear is necessary to prevent injury. Hockey and football players wear shoulder pads, hip and thigh pads, and helmets, as do football players. Boxers wear gloves and mouthpieces. These could all be considered the player's *armor*. This gear allows an athlete to play his best while protecting vulnerable internal organs and preventing broken bones or lost teeth.

An athlete knows there are hazards to playing a particular game. If he is not wearing his gear or forgets to put on a particular piece, he might get hurt. However, when he is finished playing, he takes off his gear, grabs a shower, and puts on clean clothes. As any amateur hockey player knows, if he wore his gear home, his wife would not let him in the door!

On the emotional level, we have protective gear or armor as well, and there is a right time and a wrong time to wear it as well. When we are on the field of life, our emotional armor guards us from being blindsided by an attack on our character; it protects our vulnerable side. Our armor consists of the words, attitudes, and actions we use in everyday life. For instance, you would not go into a job interview and

> *Emotional armor is like a sixth sense we have about people, situations or ourselves.*

tell a prospective employer about your emotional struggles. Instead, you show your good side while your armor keeps your emotions in check. If you are in the boardroom, you do not discuss last night's argument with your wife. You stick to business and shove that other stuff to the side for the time being. At the same time, you would not go home to your wife and act the same way you would in the boardroom—all business. No, that is the time to take your emotional armor off, to become vulnerable. Going home to your wife is like a boxer retreating to his corner between rounds or a hockey team going to the dressing room between periods. It is a time for intimacy, encouragement, instruction, and repairs or readjustments to your emotional armor.

Wearing our feelings on the outside all the time is like leaving our gear in the equipment bag and then stepping onto the ice in nothing but skates. It can stop us from being productive team members and leave us open to injury. We also do not open up to someone we cannot trust; someone we know would gossip or use our weaknesses against us. That is the same as forgetting to wear a piece of your armor.

Our emotional armor also allows us to be wary of people who would take advantage of us, people who would abuse or mistreat us. Have you ever had a feeling that something isn't quite right? You just do not like or trust someone but you have no real reason for it? That is your protective gear. Have you ever considered saying something about yourself but felt uneasy inside and kept your thoughts to yourself? That is your armor again.

Emotional armor is like a sixth sense we have about people, situations or ourselves. It gives us insight without the reasoning behind it. It allows us to deal with our bosses, co-workers, family members, and everyday life without coming out bloodied and beaten.

Our principles are also a form of emotional armor. They help us withstand the pressure of making bad choices that could result in emotional disaster down the road. Holding to a principle of marital fidelity, for example, is armor against a flirtation that could lead to an affair.

Nevertheless, not every piece of emotional armor is good. We put on macho "I'm cool" uniforms. We wear shoulder pads made out of barbed words and then smash our wives and kids into the boards. We put on our "It's my way or the highway" helmets, put our heads down, and charge, refusing to listen to anyone else. Negative gear forms the emotional barriers we put up such as self-focus and self-importance and behavioral barriers, such as avoidance and listening without empathy.

This negative armor is hard to take off. We might have put it on after being wounded by trauma as children, and we are used to wearing it. We may think it is part of our personality or makeup when in fact it is shielding us from who we really are and stunting our growth. When we wear this stuff, we run roughshod through life and over people, thinking we are safe and protected. But the opposite is true. Eventually, it will cause us to break a leg, separate a shoulder, or lose a few teeth while causing collateral damage to those we love.

TAKING IT OFF

Learning when to wear the proper gear is of utmost importance to your emotional well being. It is okay to trust your instincts about someone or a particular situation. Time will tell whether you are right, so it is better to wait rather than rush into something. C-Zone men can be too trusting; they spill their guts to people they have only just met. If you do this, you may think that you are just being open and trusting, like you are supposed to be. In fact, you are showing how wounded you are. You are saying, "I'm broken and hurt. I need someone to accept and love me the way I am. I do not care who does this, as long as someone does." Being this open with people you do not know—or those who do not give a rip about you—often sets you up for further damage.

Even when it comes to people you trust and want to be open with, there are proper times and ways to do so. You have to know the other person and the strength of your relationship.

MY MEN'S GROUP

One of the best places to find out what type of protective gear you are wearing is in a men's group. This group is like a team in the locker room after a game. The sticks are in the corner, and we are all sitting on benches, discussing the game in which we just played our hearts out. We may be bruised and bloodied, but we all have stories to tell.

It takes guts to remove your protective gear in a group.

In our men's group, we talk about the game of life. We leave our weapons (macho images, caustic words, competitive impulses, etc.) at the door, and we take our seats on the bench, and then strip off our protective gear. Underneath our sweat and blood, we often find wounds. We use empathy—our own experiences and victories—and prayer to help heal one another's injuries. We help each other understand the difference between negative and positive emotional gear and issue challenges to get rid of the negative stuff so that we can respond to life and relationships in healthy ways. When we put our protective gear back on, we exchange the negative for the positive, giving us a new perspective on life.

It takes guts to remove your protective gear in a group like this. Often, we fear being discovered as a fraud as the facades we have built so carefully are torn away. When we are vulnerable, we want to make sure those around us are on our team. We do not want to face ridicule. We need people who are supportive. Safety, therefore, is critical to this process.

HOW TO CREATE SAFETY

For any team to be successful, it needs to foster an atmosphere of solidarity. A men's group must do the same. A good one will have:

• A safe and comfortable environment where everyone can follow his individualized emotional workout program, using the appropriate

equipment—such as books, tapes, a list of pertinent conferences or workshops, and group member phone numbers
- A routine—a consistent time and meeting place
- Guidance supplied by others who are more experienced or who have gone through the same issues we are facing
- A sense of what works and what does not. Sometimes, trial and error is the only way we can learn what does and does not work for us. Other times, those around us can show us easier ways to work out our emotions and offer practical help.

When you join a men's group, you need to check your defense mechanisms and destructive emotional weapons at the gym door. Leave judgment, blame, criticism, resentment, and contempt in your gym bag and stuff it in your locker. For once, pat yourself on the back for forgetting the combination!

In men's groups, men open up and reveal things that will surprise you, not because they are so shockingly different but because they are so shockingly *the same*. You will find yourself identifying with the man who is sharing his inner journey. You will care about him. And when you do, you will find it much easier to have compassion for yourself when confronting your own weaknesses.

> *When you join a men's group, you need to check your defense mechanisms and destructive emotional weapons at the gym door.*

One thing is for sure: It is too easy for men to fall into superficial discussions and not deal with their stuff. Men's group meetings are too important to waste on watered-down talk. This is the time to get real, so do not waste it. Find out who you really are, your strengths and weaknesses, and start working out with your buddies.

CHAPTER 8:

FINDING A COACH

THE SEARCH

If you played Little League baseball or soccer as a kid, imagine what the game would have been like if there had been no coach to show you the rules, teach you how to throw the ball or explain how to dribble it down the field with your feet. Imagine what your game would have been like if no expert had corrected you when you were on the verge of developing bad habits. In any sport, bad form leads to injuries.

As I mentioned, when writing this book I looked for a fitness coach to better understand the parallels between emotional and physical fitness. Getting in peak physical condition would be a bonus to the writing process. But finding a good coach was not easy.

I drove to a nearby fitness center, planning to sign up with a coach. A sandy-haired woman in her twenties gave me a tour of the facilities then brought me to a neat, well-organized office.

"What are your goals?" She asked, clipboard in hand.

"I want to know what's possible before I set goals," I said. "I want my goals to be realistic." The interview continued. Though she was fit and well educated, she asked me clumsy questions that were more like statements thrown out in a haphazard fashion. She hoped that I would latch on to one, saying, "That's it! That is what I want to do!"

I needed a program to help me get into better shape. I needed accountability so I would not drop out midstream when things got tough. I also needed to make sure I would not hurt myself by going too fast, working out too hard or lifting weights that were too heavy. But what could I aim for? I did not know what fitness goals were possible. This experience made me realize that a good coach or trainer will not only help you reach goals, he or she will also help you *set* your goals. Unfortunately, this pleasant young woman did not help me with that.

THE FIND

Resisting the urge to give up, I found out about a former Toronto Argonauts football player who now worked as a personal trainer. He was at the other extreme end of the spectrum. Chris Munford was choosy about his clientele, and he was not cheap. We met at a restaurant to size each other up. Man, was he fit! But his knowledge of fitness impressed me even more than his physique.

"It's better to work out in your home," Chris said. "I want to show you how to develop a daily physical fitness routine. I want to change your lifestyle."

Hmm, that is a good emotional fitness principle, I thought. So I hired Chris, and he came by three times a week to help me work out. He was tough, but I grew stronger and learned a great deal as a result of his tutelage. That is what you want from your emotional coach as well. You want someone who will challenge you, help you change your lifestyle and show you the way, because they have already traveled the path you are on.

EXPERIENCE COUNTS

It is always good practice to consult with an expert, whether in sports, business or leading an outstanding life. For example, when starting a business, I meet with a chartered accountant to make sure the financial plan is solid. When needing legal advice I meet with a lawyer. Over the years, the practice of finding coaches or mentors has helped me grow in wisdom and character. Whether it is in the emotional or physical arena, if you really want to improve your game, you need find a good coach. If you really want to grow, you need to model yourself after someone who has proven skills in the areas you desire to improve in yourself.

Ideally, your coach will be someone who has already won some trophies in the emotional fitness area and has a proven track record in finishing well. Do not rely just on what this person tells you about himself. Ask others, especially his wife and children, about him. For most of us, it is easy to wear an "I've got it together" mask in public. You are looking for a coach who is a man of integrity—the same inside as outside. Look for a coach who knows how to maintain good boundaries. A good mentor will not allow you to become emotionally dependent on him, but, like a good father, he will help you find the best ways for you to build your own emotional strength. He will encourage you to develop good habits.

If you really want to grow, you need to model yourself after someone who has proven skills in the areas you desire to improve in yourself.

If you have no one like that in your life right now, choose one of your workout buddies, one with a good, reliable character. Offer to coach him in return in areas where you are strong, and make this an accountability relationship. That means you will hold each other to standards you set for yourselves and give each other permission to speak honestly about how each of you is measuring up.

A good coach ensures the terms of the coaching contract are understood. Will the relationship be more about guidance, accountability or both? You will identify and review short and long-term goals together regularly and agree on ways to identify success. Your coach should understand your challenges and help you create a solid plan of action. He will maximize your learning and be committed to his own growth as well. He will walk the talk, and he will help you do the same.

TRI-TRAINING

When Chris started making his house calls, some of the sessions included an exercise where I stood on one foot, eyes closed, lifting a weight at the same time.

"This will tune your balance," he said. "You will be ready to respond instinctively without getting thrown off."

I was surprised that Chris spent so much time having me work on exercises designed to strengthen the inner core of my body. Balance training was part of that, as were exercises targeted at strengthening abdominal and back muscles. He explained that when your core muscles are strong, you can do so much more without risking injury or getting thrown off balance.

Core, *strength*, and *endurance*: These are the three pillars of physical fitness, and a good trainer will get you to work out in all three areas. This is called *tri-training*.

Emotional tri-training is much the same. It is possible to isolate and work on one aspect of the emotions. However, we need balance, strength, and endurance to be whole. Sometimes we isolate an area and work on that, but for maximum fitness, an athlete needs to work out all three areas.

EMOTIONAL GYM EQUIPMENT

A good trainer also helps to ensure that you are working out with the right amount of resistance. We cannot just go through the motions of exercise without the resistance caused by weight or gravity or the stretching of large rubber bands. You have probably heard the saying, "No pain; no gain." What that really means is, "No resistance; no workout."

Life brings us circumstances that provide plenty of resistance—usually in the form of stress—to develop emotional strength. Unfortunately, we rarely see our various trials as an opportunity to work out. Instead, we resent them, avoid them, stuff our emotions aside, and shut down. Or we get angry and try to break the very thing that, if we responded properly, could make us stronger.

Imagine a person going to a gym and getting his exercise by watching everyone work out or by destroying all the equipment with a baseball bat. We know that gym equipment is designed to help us exercise, so we learn to use the equipment properly. Life provides us with all the equipment we need to work out our emotions. Try seeing life's stresses like equipment in a weight room. Even this small shift in your attitude will help make you stronger.

BELIEVE IN YOURSELF

When Chris and I worked together, we had a spacious area on the second floor of my barn about 100 yards from my house. I thought I was in decent physical shape already. I had worked out regularly most of my life, and tending elk demanded a lot of physical labor. However, I soon reached my limits as Chris pushed me harder and faster than I had ever pushed myself.

It amazed me how having someone standing over my shoulder, demanding that I keep at it, work harder, and go the distance, motivated me. At times, I loathed Chris's constant prodding and had to remind myself that the pain I was feeling was for my own good. It was what I was paying him for.

Nevertheless, the turmoil showed on my face.

"Stop grimacing. Relax your shoulders and neck," Chris said, "You're too tight. Concentrate on relaxing those muscles throughout your workout."

In the middle of a weight-lifting set, Chris drove me to the point of positive failure—I had reached my limit and could go no further. On the third of three sets, I could barely lift the bar. "You are looking away, turning your head, grimacing, and straining," Chris said. "Relax. Look straight ahead, not to the side. Look into your eyes."

Facing the mirror, I concentrated on my eyes. They seemed strange and harsh. Why would looking into my eyes seem so detrimental, I wondered, even while the trainer was urging me to do it? Chris said this would energize me. But as I stared at my eyes, I felt power and momentum seeping *out* of my body. I averted my gaze.

On the next set, I struggled again.

"Look into your eyes!" Chris said.

I saw harshness again. *Why am I losing energy? Why is Chris urging me to do this?*

Then the realization broke through. I remembered a time when, as a teenager, I had stared at myself in the mirror and, instead of seeing my own reflection; I saw my father's face and sensed I was gazing into my father's eyes. I recalled how I felt as a child when my father looked intently at me. I saw and felt his disapproval. I had failed. I was no good. I felt anger, confusion, a need to look away from that harsh gaze, a need to hide. Why were my own eyes making me feel the same way? And why now? I had forgiven my father long ago.

I came to the following conclusion: I know my character and myself. I know that I am changing and developing. But deep down, I can fall into a place where I do not trust myself. In those moments when Chris pushed me to the point of positive failure, I fell into that place, and I did not think I had what it took to pull myself through.

As I reflected later, I knew those feelings were not rational. I have reached the point of failure many times in my life, and I have pulled through time and again. But I also know there have been times when I have not met my own expectations, and I may not have forgiven myself. I hold onto memories that are more about my failures than my successes. At times, my belief in myself is not as strong as my belief in others or their belief in me.

My experience demonstrates that developing emotional fitness is a journey. Learning to believe in yourself will motivate you to push through the pain of tough times and help you develop the wholeness that comes through emotional balance, strength, and endurance. But it is a lifelong process, a habit to be exercised and developed over time.

EMBRACE THE EDGE

When working out with weights, a "burnout set" is designed to ensure that your muscles are maxed out with no more to give. You push them to absolute fatigue. When discovering this place of positive failure, it is amizing to find out that you are capable of doing more than you imagine. One reason we do not work to our capacity is our response to pain or exhaustion. Once we become comfortable with the feeling of working to the maximum of our strength and tuned in to how our bodies feel when we are on this edge, we can learn to embrace it, to, as Chris says, "enjoy the feeling."

A good emotional fitness coach will help you understand when you reach positive failure.

Like Chris, a good emotional fitness coach will help you understand when you reach positive failure. This is your growing edge where you develop a different mind set, where you push through barriers that used to restrict your progress. Your coach will encourage you to welcome these painful moments because of the opportunity they provide to know yourself and find freedom. Authentic growth and development includes failure and setbacks.

Your coach can point out when you are reaching positive failure in your relationships at work or with your wife and kids. This is not the time to beat yourself up but to stop, reflect, and see how your growing edge has moved in a positive direction. Instead of cowering from these painful times, "enjoy the feeling." This may seem masochistic, but in truth, it is simply changing the way we view emotional pain. Instead of seeing it as something to dread, fear or hate, we can turn times of positive emotional failure into reflective times. If we do, we will have major growth spurts in our character building process.

DANCING LESSONS

Shortly after Chris's coaching prompted me to think about positive failure and the growing edge, I had a chance to put these principles into practice. Cathy and I had committed to taking ballroom dancing lessons as a way of spending more time together and having fun. On this particular week, however, our lessons turned into an emotional burnout set.

I am not a naturally good lead dancer. It is difficult for me to visualize the next step, and the flow of the movements does not come easily. What is intended to be a fun experience usually ends up like work, because I want to get it right.

If we are not moving in sync, I will say to Cathy, "You're not matching my moves!" The dance instructor, though, knows who is making the mistakes, and, usually, it is not my wife.

At home after this particular class, Cathy felt put out. This was supposed to be about fun and romance. Instead, our negative patterns and weaknesses showed up on the dance floor. Refusing to accept responsibility for my lack of coordination and inability to follow the instructor, I fell back into my old routine of blaming my wife.

The edge was much closer that evening, because we were both worn out from a long and tiring week. I needed to show strength, endurance, and much more flexibility. I needed to make the right choices. I didn't. When we got home, I lay down on the couch, slept through dinner, and went to bed early. Stubbornness showed up, and weakness prevailed. I kicked into avoidance and dropped the ball.

This dancing lesson episode is an example of *positive* failure. If I always dropped the ball, then I would remove the adjective "positive" from "failure." Instead, Cathy and I had been doing a lot of things right. Though busy, our week had been successful and productive. We had thrown a surprise party for our older son's eighteenth birthday. I had finished a detailed report on a consulting contract, and our twelve-year-old daughter was away in Peru on a three-week mission trip, and though we missed her, we were very proud of her.

If we lived in an ideal world, our own fathers would be our primary coaches or mentors.

But we hit the edge during that dance class and stopped our emotional dance for a while. I call this positive failure, because it established the growing edge for us. It allowed us to see how far that edge had moved and to observe our newfound strength. We could understand how our positive choices throughout out the week enabled us to get as far as we had. But we also saw new areas for potential growth. I am not excusing my behavior or my weakness. I just want to highlight that it has given me the opportunity to identify the growing edge once again.

How do I respond when I hit positive failure and discover my growing edge? First, I am thankful for discovering where it is located. Then I journal about being at this edge. (I will talk more about journaling later.) That helps me understand what it looks and feels like. That understanding allows me to strengthen my ability to push through the next time I reach positive failure. Next, I reflect on the progress I have made. Looking through my journal, I see all I have accomplished. I have made progress, and it has been good. After reflecting, I discuss my failures with my wife. I apologize for hurting her, and I reaffirm my love for her. Then I talk about it with my workout group and my coach, letting them know about this latest edge. I listen to their advice, coaching, encouragement, and instruction. Finally, I commit to learning how to be more balanced, strong, and enduring.

FATHER HUNGER

If we lived in an ideal world, our own fathers would be our primary coaches or mentors. But many of them were absent physically or emotionally. Their absence has created a *father hunger* in many of us. What is father hunger? It is the need to be affirmed, accepted, and loved by an older male authority figure, ideally our biological father. Sadly, many men grow up hungering for their father's love, acceptance, and strength. Without these things, men tend to shut down emotionally at an early age. They are hungry for their father.

Take my friend, whom I will call Pete. His father walked out on his family when Pete was ten. The emotional void and pain he felt overwhelmed him. For years, he longed to have his dad hold him, say he loved him, and that everything would be all right.

As he grew, the rawness of his emotional wounds was too painful to look at. So Pete shut down and vowed never to feel again. But, as with many men, Pete's father hunger caused his stuffed-down feelings to explode in angry outbursts and fits of rage any time someone tried to get close to him. Although he grew physically, he continued to deal with emotional issues like he was still ten years old.

Even after he married, Pete's father hunger dogged him, and his angry outbursts continued. He did not start to grow emotionally until he began meeting with a group of men. Within this safe environment, he found men who would love and accept him, and he learned the real reasons behind his anger—his hunger for a father's love. Little by little, this group of trusted men drew him out of his emotional shell and challenged him to explore his painful emotions. In many ways, they became surrogate fathers and life coaches for Pete.

Years later, Pete's wife and kids are proud to have him in their lives. Whenever his father hunger growls within him, he turns to his workout buddies and mentors to explore the reasons why and find the path to healing that he needs.

In his book *Wild at Heart*, author John Eldredge talks about how masculinity is something that is imparted or passed along, like a mantle or a cloak. He writes that, "Masculinity is bestowed by masculinity."[2] Ideally, a man's father affirms his masculine identity, and this equips him to be the best he can be. But when a man is weak because of father hunger, he does not have the emotional strength to fulfill his purpose in life. After reading Eldredge's book, I looked forward to spending time with my father.

In the summer of 2002, I arrived at our family cottage to find him sitting on his ATV. "Want to join me for a ride?" Dad asked. Dad's normal route is up and down the beach road, right in front of the cottages with their open windows and peering eyes. His normal speed approximates that of a turtle on Valium. As a forty-two-year-old male who has owned numerous motorcycles, I did not relish the prospect of sitting on the back of a glorified tricycle (though this one had four wheels for added stability) and idling up and down the beach in second gear.

"Okay, Dad, but only if you take the forest trail," I said, attempting to keep my masculine identity intact.

I got on and sat with as much of my rear on the back rack as I possibly could. I leaned backward, stabilizing myself by grasping the rack itself. I thought about the intimacy I share with my wife as she holds me tight while riding on my motorcycle. There was none of that here.

We traveled into the woods inhaling the fresh smell of the forest. The thick moss dampened the sounds of our travel. Memories of my childhood flooded my senses, memories of spending countless hours in this same forest with a pellet gun and a rapidly dwindling pack of licorice. My father showed me trees he had planted that were now tall and majestic, areas he had cleared that were now well traveled, and favorite spots that he continued to enjoy. I was overtaken by a strong connection with my childhood, a period when I spent most of my time avoiding my father. We had both come a long way. We were comfortable idling along on this private path in the woods.

I wanted to bury my head in my father's shoulder blades and weep for all the lost years, the lost time, and the misspent energy because of bitterness, anger, and confusion. He was so close, so real, and so approachable at this moment that I wanted to hug him and connect at a deep level that would erase all the pain, to cry, "Daddy," like it was my first time. I longed to fill my father hunger.

I wanted to bury my head in my father's shoulder blades and weep for all the lost years, the lost time, and the misspent energy because of bitterness, anger, and confusion.

It did not happen.

Instead, I sucked it up, as we men usually do. I did not risk putting my real feelings on my sleeve but took a long slow breath, stuffed down my emotions, and denied the compulsion that flooded my being.

I lost a healing opportunity that day, a chance to really be me. I closed a window that would let in fresh breezes of healing and bypassed an opportunity to connect.

Like me, most men are trained to bury their true feelings and avoid emotional risk unless we are the aggressors. Every day, we miss out on opportunities like this to be our authentic selves. In the following chapters, we will look at *Emotional Training Exercises* that will help you avoid such emotional dead ends so you can develop emotional strength and endurance and enjoy life to the fullest.

CHAPTER 9:

CORE TRAINING

Have you ever seen the ads on TV for machines that shoot stimulating jolts of electricity into your muscles to exercise them while you relax? You may have seen those special belts that zap your abs while you go about your day, guaranteeing you a six-pack without the sweat of doing sit-ups.

This is my advice: Keep away from quick-fix gadgets and drop the get-fit-quick mentality. In fitness and weight loss, these products offer great ways to siphon off your cash, nothing more. It is the same in the emotional fitness arena. There is no weekend seminar with a motivational speaker, no week-long retreat with the latest guru of transformation that is going to do any more than make you feel good temporarily. Permanent change in the physical or the emotional arena requires time and discipline. It is a process, not a quick fix. To become emotionally fit, you need to work out at home. As my trainer Chris told me, you must develop lasting habits, a change in lifestyle.

Do not expect someone else to make changes for you. Some people think that getting their stomachs stapled or having liposuction is the answer to their obesity. While you may get the results you want visually, you can end up an unhealthy, thinner person if the underlying poor nutrition and lack of

To become emotionally fit... you must develop lasting habits, a change in lifestyle.

exercise are not addressed. In the same way, some people pin their hopes onto a celebrity or a person they want to be like, hoping somehow that person's charisma, simple self-help slogans or breakthrough vitamin formulas will create instant transformation.

Instead of falling prey to such temptations, use your common sense and start making small incremental changes that will become part of your lifestyle. Simple things, like parking your car further away from your office or taking the stairs instead of the elevator, can have a positive effect on your fitness over time. Similarly, incorporating parallel routines into your emotional fitness program will build a healthy emotional lifestyle. In fact, by picking up this book, doing the survey, handing it out to others, and plotting your current location in the Zones, you have begun to work out already. When you find a workout buddy or make a phone call to someone you would like to have as a coach, you are working up a sweat. Remember the tri-training exercises Chris had me do: *Core, strength* and *endurance?* There are emotional exercises that parallel those three areas as well.

The object is to build emotional muscles, not walls. You need to lift burdens and reduce emotional fat by resisting the tendency to be lazy, unmotivated, and unwilling to face challenges. It is important to have a strong, well-balanced, stable core. When you build emotional muscle you will be able to take on bigger challenges, lift heavier burdens, and endure greater trials without losing your peace of mind. In addition, emotional training will help you release the anger that you are holding in your back and shoulders or the anxiety that is rumbling in your stomach. Your body and emotions are tied together.

> *Your body and emotions are tied together. As you identify with your emotions, you will understand how they manifest in your body as well.*

As you identify with your emotions, you will understand how they manifest in your body as well.

With improved strength, you will deal with your problems in a different way. You will resolve arguments faster and avoid the traps of anger and resentment. In these tri-training workouts, core exercises focus on reflection. Strength exercises focus on character-building resistance training. Endurance training gives us the strength to go the distance, to persist in the program, and to maintain our character and productivity. Keep core, strength, and endurance in mind as you tailor your individual workout program to strengthen each area.

STRETCH

Before doing any exercise, you need to warm up. This involves being honest with yourself. It means deciding to stretch emotionally when you feel stress. The more you stretch, the quicker you will lose your rigidity, and the more flexible you will become. Get ready to be real.

Chris incorporated stretching into my core exercises instead of limiting it to warm-up and cool-down times. He called it "active stretching." Active stretching warms and loosens up the body to prepare for exercise. A properly warmed-up body will be more functional, more efficient, and less prone to injury.

Here is an example of active stretching. Chris told me to close my eyes and lunge, dropping down on one leg with twenty-pound weights in my hands. With eyes closed, I stretched my arms in three different directions: twelve o'clock, three o'clock, and five o'clock. Then I would have to push back up to balance on one leg. It was a huge challenge to my core, stomach, and back muscles to balance on one leg, flexing, yet stretching at the same time. When I am with a group of committed guys, I feel challenged and stretched in the same way.

You stretch with every emotional exercise you do. They all require you to go into terrain that can feel as scary and exhilarating as rappelling down a rock face for the first time. Make a practice of pushing yourself out of your comfort zone every day. Do something that is uncomfortable or new as frequently as possible. It could be volunteering to give a speech or visiting an acquaintance in the hospital. The point is to get out of your comfort zone, to stretch. Reach for your dreams. Get the emotional blood flowing. Breathe in that oxygen and stretch some more. You will function better, be less prone to emotional injury, and put your emotional growth on the fast track.

CENTRED MOVEMENT

Working on your core—your character—requires choosing to enter the Being Zone, *the reflective zone.*

Chris explained that every movement I make must come from my center, as if there's a firing mechanism inside. We focused on balance, stretching, proper relaxation, and exercises to strengthen the core muscles of the abdomen and back. Working on your core—your character—requires choosing to enter the *Being Zone,* the reflective zone. In the B-Zone, you will learn to balance, stretch, relax, and exercise through reflection. The following exercises will strengthen your core. Maybe you are already doing some of them. Congratulations! It means you are paying attention to your inner man, your soul. The core exercises focus on our ability to be our true self. Let's get started!

CORE EXERCISES

KEEP A RECORD

If you join a fitness club and start weight training, usually, you receive a sheet of paper with columns in which you list each machine, the settings you use, and the weights you are lifting on each one. You are supposed to fill in the sheet every time you work out so you can track the weights you use for your triceps, biceps, shoulders, quads, hamstrings, and so on. This gives you a benchmark for your progress. You can see at a glance what you started lifting, what you lifted the last time, and how your strength is increasing over time. You need to do the same thing with your emotional workouts.

Many of the core, strength, and endurance exercises will have added power and benefit if you write them down. You will be tracking your emotional progress the same way you would track your weight training. In your emotional workout, the act of keeping this record is a key core exercise.

Buy a notebook. It does not matter if it is a simple spiral bound one or a leather-bound journal. Find one that fits you. Remember to date your journal entries. Your notebook is a blueprint of your personal time in the *Being Zone*. It is the place to catalogue the activities in your inner gymnasium.

SCHEDULE B-ZONE TIME

Set aside time for quiet reflection in the morning before everyone else gets up and/or before you go to bed at night. Use this time for a variety of core exercises. Find a time that works best for you. Perhaps you can take ten minutes during your lunch hour to write in your journal or to sit quietly without an agenda.

Whatever you do, start small. Even if you commit to only five minutes a day, that is better than an hour today and then nothing the rest of the month. I have seen too many guys enter the gym hyped up and ready to spend hours building their bodies only to disappear a few weeks later. If you start with a short amount of time on a regular basis and add to it slowly, you will not flame out.

If you start with a short amount of time on a regular basis and add to it slowly, you will not flame out.

129

Establish a pattern of reflection into your day by scheduling your *Being Zone* time on your calendar or electronic organizer. Scheduled time will serve you far better than trying to enter the B-Zone after a crisis or after you have lost your temper and cannot calm down. It will help you maintain your inner peace in the face of provocation or confrontations that would normally make your blood boil. Through scheduling, you are preparing in advance for the inevitable crises that you will face. When you are strong, you will handle them with confidence.

DO REGULAR ZONE CHECK-UPS

In your B-Zone time and regularly throughout the day, assess where you are in terms of the Zones. Are you in the *Destructive Zone?* The *Can't Zone?* Sometimes, merely taking time to enter the *Being Zone* and reflect is enough to help you come out of C or D.

Use the Zones the way you might periodically check your pulse to measure your heart rate. You could set the alarm on your watch for every couple of hours to do a Zone check-up. What Zone are you in? How did you get there, by choice or by accident? Where do you want to be? What must you do to get there? If you take even a few moments several times a day to stop and assess objectively how you are doing, you are working out. You can do this while commuting to work, taking a shower or doing household chores that do not require your full attention.

PRAY OFTEN

Studies have shown that people who pray regularly generally lead happier, healthier lives. They also live longer than those who do not pray. Prayer has been shown to have a positive impact on people with a variety of illnesses. It can lower your blood pressure, promote healing, and improve your brain chemistry in ways that help your emotional well being.

If you have a spiritual tradition, dust off what you were taught about prayer and start putting it into practice. Prayer can be simple and honest. For example, "Help me, please!" is a prayer. Again, start small and build. If you do not know what to pray, open a Bible to the Book of Psalms and find one that seems to suit your emotional state. In Psalms, you can find anger, sorrow, fear, illness, joy, and praise—the gamut of human emotion. You will be able to see in print how you feel inside.

READ MORE

Take time to read good self-help books and inspired religious teachings. Write down the words that speak to you. Target your reading to address problems you have uncovered through your understanding of the Zones. If you are living in the D-Zone most of the time, find self-help books that deal with anger. If you are in the C-Zone, search for books to help you manage anxiety and develop self-esteem. If you have difficulty sharing your feelings or your loved ones complain that you do not listen, read books on communication. Agree on a book and reading plan with your workout buddies and discuss what you are learning regularly.

SPEND TIME ALONE

Make a practice of spending time alone and devoting that time to reflection. Walk to the store instead of driving so you can carve a little solo time for yourself. When everyone is gone out for the evening, leave the TV off and enjoy the peace. Go for a walk in the woods or a drive down the highway and use the time to reflect. Try a weekend retreat or go camping alone without a radio or books.

LISTEN ACTIVELY

Few people understand the art of listening. Most of us want to reply to what is being said before the other person even finishes speaking. Instead of composing your reply, listen to your wife or child without allowing distractions—including your own thoughts—to intrude. Lots of guys *think* they are listening while they are looking at the sports page at the same time. Trust me, your wife does not feel like you are listening when you do that. Nor do your kids feel like you are paying attention to them while you are clicking the remote.

Active listening—really paying attention—takes practice and discipline. Initially, you will have to resist the urge to defend yourself or judge the other person's words. Maintain eye contact. Then just listen and observe the other person. The object is to listen without any agenda except active attention.

You will be amazed at the effect this will have on the person to whom you are listening. As with any exercise, you may find it difficult and painful at first, but with practice you will get better. Soon, this will become a habit that deepens your relationships and builds connections with others in ways that you never dreamed possible.

Few people understand the art of listening.

Two friends of mine, Brady Wilson and Alex Somos, are masters at listening. They state, "When people feel truly understood, something almost magical happens. It unlocks their capacity to understand others. Relationships become virtuous circles instead of vicious cycles." You can test your listening skills at their web site: www.juicefactor.ca.

CULTIVATE THANKFULNESS

Developing an attitude of thankfulness will affect your thought life and overall physical health. Negative thoughts release harmful chemicals in your body that contribute to many illnesses, such as depression.

Make thankfulness a discipline, especially when you do not feel thankful. Write a list of everything in your life for which you are thankful. Nothing is too big or too small. This may be difficult, but do it anyway. The emotional effect will rejuvenate you, just as a sports drink rejuvenates you when you are dehydrated. Mental fatigue and exhaustion will slip away. A new vigor will spread into your outlook. Whenever you fall back into your "stinking thinking," you will be able to resist it with your thankfulness list.

RELATIONSHIP INVENTORY

One exercise that I often recommend to those I coach is a relationship inventory. This is where you take stock of your beneficial and destructive relationships. To do this exercise, fill in the diagram below, starting with the column on the left. Write down the names of your wife or girlfriend, children, parents, siblings, and other relatives and friends with whom you have regular contact or who play a significant role in your life, either positive or negative. You can also include relationships in your work life as well, such as leaders, team members, clients or customers.

Now, take a look at the rest of the diagram. The first column to the right of the names has a "plus" sign over it (+). Put a check mark or an "X" next to the names of anyone, who encourages you, builds you up, helps you or gives you more than you give back.

The next column has a "plus/minus" (+/-) sign over it. Put a mark

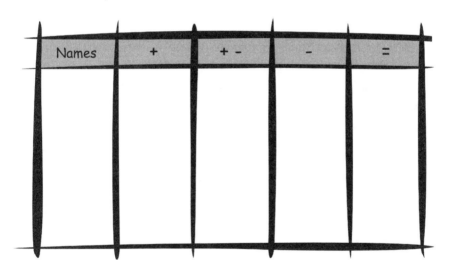

Names	+	+ -	-	=

in that column next to each person to whom you give more than you receive, but doing so has a positive effect on your life. As a good father, you give to your children, so they would be included in this column. If you coach or mentor someone, put a mark beside his or her name. The plus comes in the rewards for giving to others or in discharging your responsibilities to others faithfully.

> *You become like those you hang around with, so upgrade your friends as you resolve to upgrade your character.*

The next column has a "minus" (-) sign over it. Survey your list of people who have a negative effect on you, who drain you by taking but never giving back. These are the toxic people in your life. They are the ones who bring you down, who encourage your bad habits or sabotage your self-confidence. Maybe they are your drinking buddies or the ones with whom you play golf or hockey. They could also be your parents or siblings. These people do not improve or change when you give to them. In the (-) column, put a mark next to each person on your list that falls into this category.

In some relationships, the giving and taking are equal. If you have a friend like that, you might feel that you would give him the shirt off your back and vice versa. That is the column on the far right with an "equal" (=) sign at the top. Put a mark next to those names where your relationships are reciprocal.

Now, take an overall look at your inventory. How many pluses do you have? How many plus/minuses? Minuses? Equal signs? If you are low in the plus column and high in the minus column, you associate with too many people who drain you. If you do not have any plus/minus relationships, then you are not giving back enough.

Once you have reflected on your relationship inventory, try this strength training exercise: Find more relationships to add to your plus column. Another exercise is to choose to spend less and less time with those who drag you down. This is a tough one. These people will not understand why you are changing your ways. They will want you to continue your bad habits so they will be more comfortable in theirs. They may even spread rumors about you or hate you for what they perceive as you "dumping" them. However, if you resolve to develop positive relationships and character, you will be able to overlook such pettiness.

You become like those you hang around with, so upgrade your friends as you resolve to upgrade your character.

CALENDAR INVENTORY

Write out a sample schedule of how you spend each hour of the day. First, take a look at your leisure time. How much time do you spend watching television or reading the sports page? Are you spending your evenings and weekends driving your kids to the hockey arena or soccer? Do you pull your weight when it comes to chores around the house? Are there ways to free some of your time for working out emotionally? Are you getting enough physical exercise?

Now, examine your time at work. How have you organized your day? Are you running around fighting fires all the time, ricocheting from one emergency to the next? Do you have every second crammed full of appointments? Are there steps you could take to prevent these fires? Do you find that you are allowing the phone and e-mail to throw you off task? Can you group your phone calls and e-mails instead of jumping from one thing to the next? Another way to do a calendar inventory is to write down everything you do on a daily basis for two weeks. This will give you a detailed picture of your lifestyle and what you perceive as important.

Think about what your calendar says about your priorities. Are you spending enough quality time with your spouse? Your children? Are you setting aside time in the day for personal growth and quiet reflection? Can you rearrange your schedule to make sure that you spend more time in the B-Zone and meeting with other men? In your busy lifestyle, something has got to give. What can you do more efficiently? What can you drop? Are you finding that you need to engage in mindless diversion because you are exhausted by frenetic activity? Could you build in some planning that will save precious time?

When we try to accomplish too much by filling up our schedules or trying to maintain relationships that are costing us emotional energy, it is like heading off on a canoe trip with too much camping gear in the boat. The canoe sinks low into the water, and there is not enough freeboard. On a calm day, this may be worth the risk, but if the winds pick up or a sudden movement causes a small shift in weight, water quickly pours over the gunnels and capsizes the canoe. Having appropriate freeboard is critical in your time management as well, because life is rarely as smooth as a lake on a calm day.

MANAGE YOUR TIME

Once you have reflected on how you use your time, create a schedule for the ideal week. Envision how each day of that week will go. Include everything that is important to you. (Careful: you may have to change your priorities.) Displace time-wasting activities with time spent on personal growth. Resolve, for example, to cut half an hour of TV each evening and devote the time to reading a good book or to quiet reflection. Little by little, increase the amount of time that you displace. Remember the canoe analogy. Start throwing out some of that excess gear so you will not capsize if the wind picks up and waves start to buffet you.

Displace time-wasting activities with time spent on personal growth.

You will start seeing the benefits if you maintain this practice over time. A word of warning to C and D-Zone guys: Do not make your new schedule a set-in-stone document. Keep your schedule flexible enough to allow for important interruptions, such as your wife needing time to talk or your kids wanting to play catch.

YOUR HEALTH

Looking after your physical health is another core exercise. Making sure you get proper exercise, nutrition, and sleep are no-brainers not only for your body but also for your emotional well being. The trouble is, most of us lead sedentary but stress-filled lives, we overeat, and we suffer sleep deprivation.

If you are serious about building your emotional health, it is necessary to change your exercise, eating, and sleeping habits. Discuss these areas with your workout buddies or coach, then set up a plan to integrate the necessary changes. Consider your physical fitness routines, a healthy diet, and regular rest as core emotional fitness exercises.

There is no doubt that a regular physical regimen will have an impact on your emotional strength and endurance. If you are neglecting your body, your body—and your mind—will neglect you.

Your lungs' ability to absorb oxygen and your heart's capacity to pump oxygen-rich blood throughout your body are critical to a healthy life, so pay attention to your cardiovascular fitness. Walking, running, swimming, and biking are excellent ways to get the heart pumping and the lungs working harder.

Eliminate junk food. It slows your body down and dulls your mind. Some foods are known to be good for fighting cancer, improving memory, and strengthening the immune system. Research what is good for you and incorporate these into your diet.

Avoid overeating. It takes twenty minutes for your body to realize your stomach is full, so stop eating before you feel stuffed. Give your stomach a chance to tell your mind that it is satisfied. Snack on healthy foods. This will enable you to eat less at those big meals where you tend to overindulge.

Get the sleep you know you need. All of us have varying lengths of sleep cycles. Deep sleep is the most restful. Some of us cycle into deep sleep and out again in two and a half hours, others in four. Most of us are somewhere in between. Track your bedtime, and set your alarm to get up ten minutes earlier each day, until you find the time that you wake up feeling most refreshed. It will probably be eight hours or a little less. Divide this time by two, and this is most likely your sleep cycle.

I have experimented with this and have found that my cycle is three-and-one-half hours. I know that I need seven hours of sleep to feel refreshed. I have also noted that my wife's sleep cycle is four hours. This means that she will need to catch a whole hour of shuteye more than I do on a regular basis. It does me good to help her with this by tiptoeing out of the bedroom early in the morning.

CHAPTER 10:

DEVELOPING
STRENGTH

In the fitness world, strength training is also called "resistance train-ing." You can use free weights or machines to develop your arms or to work on your legs, abs, back, shoulders, and so forth. Some forms of exercise, such as isometrics, call for using your own body as resistance. We are going to use this same principle of resistance to develop emotional strength.

When it comes to emotional fitness, instead of using your body or weight machines as resistance, you resist your bad habits by delib-erately going against your natural inclinations and reactions. As you resist your tendencies to judge, criticize, withhold forgiveness, condemn yourself, and so on, you will grow stronger emotionally.

The strength routines that follow build on the core exercises in the previous chapter. The core work-out will help you become aware of your thoughts and feelings in

Instead of using your body or weight machines as resistance, you resist your bad habits by deliberately going against your natural inclinations and reactions.

a new way. For instance, you might see that you constantly think critical thoughts about your wife or children. You may realize that you unload on them in lectures that alienate them and wound their souls. You might uncover a judgmental streak and find you rarely have a positive thought about anyone. You may discover anger and resentment or worry and anxiety. If so, do not get discouraged!

When you enter the reflective *Being Zone* through your core exercises, the negative thoughts and feelings you discover become the array of free weights and workout machines in your B-Zone gym. By using these tools for resistance, you will become strong. Shadowy thoughts and feelings play a huge role in how we feel and behave. We think, "out of sight, out of mind," when, in fact, keeping them in the shadows gives them far more control over us.

A JOURNAL ENTRY: SHADOW BOXING

It is Valentines Day, and I'm up at 6 a.m. After my regular quiet time, my fitness trainer, Chris, shows up. This morning's session is going to be in the barn. We're going to go over the basics of boxing as a form for my workout today.

After a quick warm-up on the stationary bike, we take a brisk walk to the barn. It is −12° Celsius [about −15° Fahrenheit], and the snow is crunching under our running shoes.

Once in the barn, it is on with the gloves and a lesson in how to punch from the hips. It is important to be centered. To keep the hands high and close, protecting the head, elbows in, protecting the body. Back and forth and around the barn floor we spar.

Often the enemies we fight are inner voices that reach out from the dark and cold, tripping us up whenever we are close to success. These voices are programmed in our youth, and we often encourage them by repeating their message to ourselves, often out loud. "I'm no good." "I'm such an idiot." "I'll never be successful."

It is important to deal with these voices. To protect our minds and our hearts form the negative messages that can derail us.

It is time to start boxing those shadows. First, start resisting the bait these thoughts and feelings offer. Next, replace the negative thoughts with truths or affirmations that contradict them. In fact, you may even want to create a two-column chart in your journal. Title the left column "Lies I believe" and the right column "Truths that refute them." Then list every lie you believe and counter it with a truth or affirmation. By doing this, you are lifting weights in addition to using your own body as resistance. Finally, change your actions to build strength in new areas of productivity and selfless giving toward others.

STRENGTH EXERCISES

RESIST

Count to Ten

If you have ever counted to ten before reacting after someone has angered you, then you have already performed one of the most well known emotional exercises on the planet. The idea is not to count to ten and then explode. Those ten seconds give you time to slow down, and reflect on a wise and appropriate response.

So your first strength exercise is resolving to resist your anger for a minimum of ten seconds. As you build strength, increase the number of seconds. Most people have only used the ten-second count when they are furious and ready to blow their stack. Do not wait until that happens. Look for small opportunities to resist annoyance and irritation, such as counting to ten when you are stuck behind a slowpoke in the fast lane or your child wastes time while getting ready for school.

Resist Judging Others

An emotional outburst of contempt or resentment often accompanies judgmental thoughts, especially toward people who stress you out. If you have the upper hand, you may feel disdain for the weaker person. If you are the weaker one, you may resent the stronger person.

Judgments usually have emotional baggage attached. You may discover that what you dislike most in others is what you refuse to accept about yourself.

Resentment and contempt create an emotional buzz; a little rush of energy like a high one might get from taking a drug. Resist that buzz by observing the bait being offered to you. When you resent someone, you are secretly feeling morally superior. You are telling yourself, "I'd never do such a thing." That is useless C-Zone self-righteousness that you hide behind as you allow people to walk all over you. Resentment lets you hide from the fact that you lack the inner strength to stand up for yourself and your principles. Contempt plays a similar role for the D-Zone man, except he uses the weakness of others to excuse his bullying and impatience.

Do not confuse judgment and discernment; they are two different things. When you judge, you take it upon yourself to decide who is good or evil. Judging also involves comparing yourself to others. You slam someone down to make yourself feel better or superior; or you cut yourself down, making yourself feel worse. Discernment gives you insight into what is really going on, without all the emotional filters. It helps you understand someone's true character. Judgments usually have emotional baggage attached. You may discover that what you dislike most in others is what you refuse to accept about yourself. You may be reacting negatively to something in a person that reminds you of past hurts. When we judge, we jump to conclusions that are often wrong.

When you stop judging, you will find that you see things in a clearer perspective. It is as if the Light of Truth I described earlier gives you insight and wisdom. Judging blocks that Light.

Do this exercise as many times a day as necessary. Persist by continually digging for the root reasons why you judge and criticize others. You will be amazed at how even this one simple exercise of resisting your tendency to judge, practiced over time, can change your life dramatically for the better.

Watch out for positive judgments, too. C-Zone men are especially vulnerable to making hasty positive judgments that prove false. Be wary when someone impresses you with how wonderful they are. Do not make that judgment. Wait, watch, and listen. Observe yourself and your reactions. Do not jump to positive or negative conclusions. Resist the impulse to pour your heart out to someone who makes a good impression on you. You will save yourself much grief by not confiding too soon in the wrong people.

Resist Condemning Yourself

You may find that you frequently tell yourself: "What a loser!" "I'm an idiot!" or "How could I be so stupid?" Such self-hatred stems from failing to stand up for yourself or indulging in bad habits. Apply ten seconds of resistance at first, resisting negative self-judgments. Keep extending this time until your habits of self-condemnation lose their power.

Imagine a long-distance runner taking out a whip and flagellating himself in order to go greater distances. Think of the energy he is wasting and the damage he is doing to himself. That is what hating and condemning yourself is like. Give

Give yourself permission to make mistakes. Tell yourself, "I messed up, but that is okay. I'm going to learn from my mistakes."

143

yourself permission to make mistakes. Tell yourself, "I messed up, but that's okay. I'm going to learn from my mistakes."

Resist the temptation to beat yourself up. You may find self-condemnation has become a compulsion. Resist, observe, and stand back. Disagree with your self-hating thoughts.

During your B-Zone time, you may discover these thoughts sound like someone from your past who laid negative messages on you continually. Often, just observing quietly and choosing not to agree with them will be enough to loosen their hold over you. Keep resisting and, eventually, you will find they do not bother you anymore. As you stop judging other people, you will find it easier to stop judging yourself. The more you judge others, the more those judgments boomerang back to you.

Resist Blame

When angry or hurt, we often blame the person who made us feel that way. "It is the other guy's fault. She provoked my anger," we tell ourselves. "Our emotions aren't the problem. It is the other person who must change."

I have news for you: You can decide how you respond to every circumstance in your life. You can choose to let something make you angry or hurt your feelings or you can choose to let those emotional darts glance off you. It takes practice in the sparring ring and lots of resistance training to get to the point where you are shielding yourself effectively from life's blows. The first step, however, is to stop blaming other people, bad luck, your job, the weather, or anything else for how you feel. Resist the tendency to blame. Take responsibility for your emotional state. Choose to act rather than react.

> *Resist the tendency to blame. Take responsibility for your emotional state. Choose to act rather than react.*

Sometimes a person will knock you flat with an unintentional blow. He was not watching where he was going. She made a joke that cut you deeply. He broke a promise. She broke a trust. Other times a person may hurt you deliberately. It is important to look at motives and confront people when and if needed. However, whether a blow is intended to hurt you or not, on an internal level you deal with it the same way. You choose how you are going to respond.

Your strength training includes not allowing anger and blame to control you. Do not give someone who is trying to upset you deliberately the satisfaction of "getting your goat." Your anger does not hurt them; neither does your blame. It only hurts you. There is an old saying, "Do not get mad; get even." I am not advocating revenge, but righting wrongs. You need to stand up for yourself, but do not use anger's negative energy to do so. Stand up for yourself out of a calm sense of justice and emotional strength.

Push Through

To grow stronger physically, you need to stress your body through using heavier weights, more repetitions, and tougher aerobic workouts. This forces your body to adapt to new levels of activity and resistance. Instead of falling back to easier routines, you push through the fatigue and the aching muscles. The same principle applies in your emotional workout. When you hit a wall of anxiety, negative feelings, anger or hurt, keep on going. Push through to the B-Zone.

It is easy to stop working out and seek diversion, but your feelings are there to make you aware of what you have been running away from through too much work, television, beer or junk

> *Stand up for yourself out of a calm sense of justice and emotional strength.*

145

food. Whatever you do, do not drop your exercise program. You will only halt your progress if you do.

Keep your eyes focused on the inner peace and strength you will experience when you have passed through this barrier. Persevere. Think of these negative emotions as the toxins your body releases when you sweat. Sometimes the cleansing process is painful, but you will feel so much better when you have eliminated the poisons from your emotions and thought life.

REPLACE

Now that you have been resisting your negative thoughts, feelings, and bad habits, it is time to move to the next level. You are going to "lift" positive truths, emotions and good habits to replace negative ones you have been resisting. In keeping with the physical fitness analogy, no longer are you using merely your own body as resistance, you are moving on to the weight machines where you will start seeing results fast.

Show Gratitude

The first weight has "gratitude" written on its side. It is heavy if you are used to grumbling or seeing the negative side most of the time. If you have started to develop thankfulness during your core workout, increase the weight by adding gratitude throughout your day. Look for genuinely positive things to think about and to say to people in your sphere, especially your wife and kids. Do not assume that people know how much you appreciate them. When you start voicing your gratitude and showing it in your face and through your gestures, you will become like a genuine athlete.

Choose to Forgive

This is a twofold weightlifting exercise. First, it is important to develop a habit of *choosing to forgive* anyone who offends you. This does not mean that you give in to, appease or deny a person's true character and actions. It does not mean you are going to be a doormat either. It means that you choose not to let their actions control you. You choose not to let them get a rise out of you. You choose not to hold a grudge or take steps to get even. The best known Christian prayer, the Lord's Prayer, says, "Forgive us our trespasses, as we forgive those who trespass against us" (Matthew 6:12).

> *By choosing to forgive, we free ourselves from emotional bondage.*

How do you do this? You learn to separate the person from the behavior. The behavior may have hurt or angered you, but this does not mean you should define the other person by his or her behavior. It is okay to let that person know that what they did was not right or that it hurt or angered you, but choose to forgive whether or not he or she is sorry.

Forgiveness is vital, because by choosing to forgive, we free ourselves from emotional bondage. If we do not forgive, we are allowing other people to hold the keys that keep us bound to the pain they caused us. Holding a grudge is like walking around in brace or a cast that has been designed improperly. Instead of correcting your posture or broken bone, it prevents the injury from healing properly. The cast of unforgiveness leaves you emotionally misshapen as long as you choose to wear it. Forgiveness is like a buzz saw that cuts off the cast and sets you free.

The second aspect of this strengthening exercise is to write down the names of people who have hurt or angered you in the past. Then, choose to forgive them one-by-one. Write down the words or deeds you have forgiven. Speak you forgiveness out loud if necessary. Speaking out loud sends a message to your subconscious that you are serious about forgiving.

Note: Forgiving someone does not mean you have to trust him or her again. There is a big difference between forgiveness and trust. Forgiveness means you let go of the past. Trust has to do with future behavior. If someone has caused you major damage and is likely to do similar things in the future, you do not necessarily have to trust him or her. But you should forgive that person for *your* own good.

Do not worry about your feelings. What is important in this exercise is your will. Make the choice to forgive and then use any lingering feelings of unforgiveness for resistance training. Keep affirming that you have chosen to forgive, and, eventually, your feelings will come in line with your will. It may help to talk with your coach or workout buddies about specific instances where forgiveness is difficult.

If, after reading this, you still do not want to forgive, ask yourself why. Are you more concerned about your rights and getting even? Keep resisting your unforgiveness until you can be honest with yourself about the root cause. When you find it and let it go, you will be free of the negative hold those people and their actions have on you.

Renew Your Mind

Your mind is one of the most important weight machines you will use. Using it involves changing the way you think about others and yourself. You will choose to change the way you see things—to look on the bright side.

For instance, you can replace lies with truth. If you are prone to thinking "I'm an idiot!" recognize this lie and replace it with a positive affirmation or a truth from your spiritual tradition. Your thought life is the key to what you believe, especially about yourself. It controls what you feel and how you act. If you renew your mind, you will be transformed from a "stinking thinker" into a positive powerhouse.

Clean up the images of yourself. In your mind's eye, you may see yourself "choking" when at bat. You see yourself striking out. Anxiety builds before the real game, and, instead of improving your performance; you are more likely to strike out. In your personal life, you may have images of yourself being irritable and impatient with your children, because you have acted that way so often in the past. Instead, enter the B-Zone and rehearse seeing yourself as a kind and patient father. In your imagination, practice seeing yourself responding to your children the way you would like to respond. Just as studies show that athletes can improve their performance by mentally visualizing a perfect dive or golf swing, you can also improve your performance by using the same technique. After all, the most important sports arena in the game of life is your home.

Choose to see your possibilities, not your limitations.

Think of times when you have been at your best, and affirm that as your self-image. Visualize yourself as the person you want to be. Face your present shortcomings and failures honestly, but do not dwell on them. Do not define yourself by them any longer. Choose to see your possibilities, not your limitations. In the past, you may have defined your emotional muscles by weakness. Now your new self-definition is founded on strength. By uncovering, admitting, and working out emotionally, you will see your new character definition grow.

Think about your strengths. Dwell on the good things about yourself and others. Think on what is true and wholesome and positive. Think about how great it will feel when you act instead of react, when you choose to love instead of behaving like a puppet, jerked around by every little emotional upset. Replace "I cannot" thoughts and words with "I can." Be persistent. You did not accumulate your negative thought life in one day, so do not expect to get rid it with one workout routine. Some negative thoughts will be more challenging to overcome. Keep at it. You will be amazed at the impact that choosing to think and imagine differently will have on your character and emotional strength.

CHANGE

Join a Men's Group

It takes effort, and, therefore, strength, to find a men's group and attend the meetings regularly. Maybe you have had to start one because there are not any in your area. That is a great strength exercise. It takes initiative to do that. The "initiative muscle" is key to becoming productive. It is one of the biggest muscles in the *Actualizing Zone*.

A regular, preferably weekly, meeting with a group of guys who share your desire to work out emotionally is a key strength exercise. Knowing you have your meeting each week will help give you the incentive to do your other workout routines. You will not want to let the other guys down. In addition to the meetings, stay in touch with one or two members of the group during the week by phone or meet for coffee.

See the Problem

In the *Actualizing Zone*, a man can separate people from the problems they face. If you have worked out by resisting judgment, blame, and criticism, you will be able to identify ways to overcome problems without harming the person who is struggling with them. If negative thoughts and feelings toward that person cloud your mind, then you are part of his or her problem.

In this strengthening exercise, you are going to do what is best for others. You will work at separating the problem from the person, even if makes you sweat big time. Start doing this with your wife and kids, and then put it into practice at work. When you have compassion for someone laboring under a problem, then you have earned the right to step in and help.

Let Go

Men stuck in the D-Zone can often be characterized as control freaks. They hover over people's shoulders and become impatient if others do not do things the way they would do them. They hound their kids, harping on every little mistake. They are not willing to allow others to mess up. They expect people to ask, "How high?" when told to jump. This strength exercise centers on dropping the baton of control

Here is the key: The only person you can change is yourself. Stop trying to change other people. Your efforts have been unwelcome. They produce outright rebellion or passive-aggressive conformity. Either way, your efforts to change others saps the joy out of family life and leeches productivity from the workplace. Instead of trying to force, coerce or impose your will upon others, lead by example. Model strength. Show servant leadership. Ask if your wife wants a solution to her problem or if she just needs you to listen. Allow your kids to make mistakes, but be ready to help when asked. Maybe your control-freak behavior has made the problem worse. Maybe it has bound the person to the problem. Here is an example: Your kid gets a bad grade in math. "You're an idiot!" You say. "Why can't you do better? If you do not pick up your grades, you'll be in big trouble." Your kid thinks: *My dad hates me. I'm no good. I'll never please him or live up to his expectations.* Throughout the next semester, he will be preoccupied by your threats and will be unable to concentrate. Thus, he fails to improve his grade—and it is partly your fault.

Let go of the desire to control, and trust that love and compassion can do the work that you, in your emotional weakness, cannot do.

However, if you separate the bad math grade from your son and work with him to find ways to improve, your relationship will grow stronger, and his grade is more likely to go up. Let go of the desire to control, and trust that love and compassion can do the work that you, in your emotional weakness, cannot do.

Apologize

This is an excellent strength exercise. But beware—it is a lot harder than it looks. It means admitting you are wrong. It means saying that you are sorry for what you have done, without making excuses, without blaming. It means listening without judgment and without trying to defend yourself when the person you have wronged lets you know how much you hurt or angered him or her. Being man enough to apologize quickly when you have messed up is a sign of strength. Genuine apologies show

> *Being man enough to apologize quickly when you have messed up is a sign of strength.*

"muscular definition" and integrity. Be careful that you do not go overboard and apologize for everything though. Some C-Zone men might apologize to get people off their backs. A *genuine* apology is neither self-serving nor manipulative.

Ask for Help

Asking for help before you have a full-blown crisis on your hands is another key strength exercise. The big resistance factor to seeking help is pride, especially if you are in the D-Zone.

D-Zone guys are like the stereotypical male drivers who get lost but refuse to ask for directions. "God helps those who help themselves," is one of their favorite slogans, although I have never been able to find that particular phrase in the Bible! D-Zone men have trouble listening to others, though they often like dispensing advice.

By asking for help, you are revealing your weaknesses. That is why this exercise is so hard. Yet, it is only through disclosing your weaknesses with someone trustworthy that you begin to build strength.

Men stuck in the C-Zone are likely to ask for help from the wrong people. Often, they ask someone who sends them off on a wild goose chase. After many such experiences, they are afraid of "help" because of how damaging it can be. Start with your workout buddies or your coach. Reach out for help, and be there to give help when others need it.

Communicate

Do not assume that because you can hear and speak that you are listening effectively or coming across clearly to others. As part of your core training, you may have started reading books on the art of communication and emotional intelligence. Now, as a strengthening exercise, try putting some of the exercises from those books into practice with your loved ones.

Remember that whenever you hear something, you filter it through your experiences and views on the subject. Many times you think that others hear the way you do. When you talk, you do so from your point of view. Start reminding yourself that the person you are conversing with may not look at life, problems or solutions the way you do.

Many good books on communication are available. Read through their suggestions. Then, in your strength training, put some of these into practice. You are already doing the active listening exercise. Here is another communication exercise: After listening carefully, summarize what the person has just told you. Ask whether your summary captures the meaning of what they just said. Listen again when the person tells you whether your summary shows that you have understood correctly.

Good communication takes time, attention, and practice. But the emotional strength you will gain by exercising in this area will be worth it. Your wife, children, friends, and co-workers will feel valued and honored by your attention. You will be amazed at how your relationships can improve with persistence in this area.

Make New Friends

In the core workout, one of the exercises was a relationship inventory. Take a look at your relationship inventory again. Do you see a huge number of minuses and few pluses in your relationship ratings? A strength exercise is to design a strategy to change the pluses into minuses on that inventory the next time you take it. This means spending less time with the negative people who showed up as minuses on your list. It means making an effort to find friends that strengthen and encourage you. Every time you lift the phone to call someone who might replace one of those people who drags you down, you are lifting a huge weight that will build emotional muscle.

You know the adage: "Like attracts like." If you do not like the team with whom you are suiting up, find a new one. Get a new uniform. Change leagues. Start hanging out with people who can teach you something about character and emotional fitness. You might feel out of place at first, but soon their lifestyle will rub off on you, and you will fit right in.

Eliminate "Should"

Have you ever noticed how you feel as soon as the words "*I should…*" leave your lips? "I should go on a diet." "I should exercise more." "I should take out my journal." "I should spend more time alone." When you say, "I should," do you feel as though you are nagging yourself or have a big finger in your back prodding you?

The word "should" creates rebellion in most of us. It makes us tired before we even start. It is like the lactic acid build-up in our muscles that makes us prefer to lie around rather than get moving. What "should" really means is you *do not want to.* You are not motivated enough to change. This exercise may surprise you: Observe every time you say the word *should* and eliminate it from your vocabulary, especially when it comes to your emotional fitness workout. One way to do this is to keep an elastic band on your wrist and snap it every time you catch yourself saying the word *should.* Your red wrist will soon show you how often that word escapes your lips. Instead of piling more guilt onto your back, think about your emotional workouts in a positive way. "I choose to exercise more." "I will take time for reflection." "I enjoy meeting with my men's group." "I feel renewed when I enter the *Being Zone.*"

> *The word "should" creates rebellion in most of us.*

Do the same thing with the words "have to." You do not *have to* work out emotionally. But you choose to do so, because you know how great you will feel when you have gained emotional strength and vitality. You choose to, because you love to grow. Replace "I should" or "I have to" with "I choose" or "I want to," and you will be amazed at how much easier it is to work out emotionally and physically.

Serve

At least once a week, do something to serve another person who may give you nothing in return. Volunteer at the local food bank or soup kitchen for an hour. Give blood. Visit a retirement home or play cards with a hospital patient who seldom has visitors. Help an elderly lady put her groceries into her trunk. Sign up to coach your daughter's soccer team. Giving without expecting anything in return is one of the best long-term, character-strengthening exercises you can do.

When you serve, make sure that you attend to the needs of the other person. Serve in a way that person would like to be served. And make sure you are giving out of the goodness of your heart, not because you want to boost your pride or soothe your conscience. C-Zone men can sometimes give too much and end up drained dry. Know when and how to say "No." Otherwise, give graciously.

Ask Others

While preparing to write this book, I interviewed many people to understand how they moved through the Emotional Zones. It was a great opportunity to ask deep, meaningful questions that most social gatherings do not permit. You may not be writing a book, but this exercise can help you, too. Call someone you admire and ask how he or she has built emotional strength and character. You will be surprised at the insights you gain. You will probably gain some new friends as well.

CHAPTER 11:

ENDURANCE TRAINING

GO THE DISTANCE

Weightlifters who only lift weights cannot run any distance because, despite their muscular physique, they have not developed cardiovascular fitness. Their bodies are strong, but they are not trained for the long haul.

In high school, I worked only on my chest, arms, and back. I looked like a chicken—a big chest and arms on skinny legs. I felt good about my muscular upper body and liked the way I looked when I walked through the halls, legs hidden inside my jeans, but I was so unbalanced that I often tripped when running.

As you set out to become emotionally fit, make sure that whether you walk, run, lift or bend, you are balanced and have the necessary endurance. Emotional strength is not just about power lifting or dealing with a crisis or two in a short period of time. We all face crises in our life. And yes, and we need strength to deal with them. But we also have to go the distance emotionally. We need the endurance of the long-distance runner. Then we can withstand long-term challenges and relational stresses. Many of us find that it is the little things that wear us down, not the big things like getting fired or getting divorced. We can muster the strength to cope when we have to. It is the day-to-day grind, the drudgery of everyday life that wears us to the bone.

Setting your mind is the first step toward building endurance. Your mindset will make or break whatever you plan to do. It takes endurance to go the distance, to keep plugging away at your emotional workout routine, especially if you do not see results right away. In fact, sometimes starting your emotional routine will make you aware of all sorts of problems you did not know you had. You might feel like things are getting worse, not better.

> *We need the endurance of the long-distance runner. Then we can withstand long-term challenges and relational stresses.*

Now that you have stopped running from your problems, you finally understand your lack of emotional fitness. If you have set your mind on a future vision of a better, stronger you, you will be able to push through these difficult times. In an emotional sense, you are going to develop arms and hands that reach out, protect, make connections, build up, help others, prevent injury, and fight the good fight when necessary. You are going to develop legs that can go the distance in relationships. You will be able to take a stand, run a difficult course, leap over obstacles, walk difficult terrain, and even kick butt when needed. You are going to develop a chest that your wife and children can lean on and strong abs and back muscles to support a firm, upright moral posture. You are going to have a balanced emotional physique, unlike the chicken-build I developed in high school.

The endurance exercises in this section involve envisioning, goal setting, and affirmations. These exercises will help you develop the strength to persist in your emotional training and motivate you to do your workouts over the long haul.

ENDURANCE EXERCISES

SHARPEN YOUR VISION

Real change does not happen in one sitting. In our world of instant gratification, fast food, and high-tech toys, we expect that once we decide to do something, it will happen instantly. Not so. Change—true change—takes time. It requires intense focus, patience, and perseverance. It takes a willingness to step into unfamiliar territory, where it may be obvious to everyone that you are a newcomer. Too often, we get set in our ways, even though we do not like the way we are. Think about this for a moment. We are willing to settle for second-best, raunchy circumstances and rotten family relationships just because they are familiar to us—definitely not a sign of emotional health.

Moving out of that safety zone can produce great conflict and anxiety. That is why so many men stay stuck in a groove. I am not suggesting here that men should leave their wives if the relationship is not working. Instead, if you work out emotionally, you may find that your wife will respond so positively that you will feel like you are honeymooning again. Envisioning success will help you focus and push through fear of failure and the sense of vulnerability. You need to imagine what it will feel like when you have reached your goal.

A good vision captures how you will feel when you accomplish something. Like a mountaineer anticipates the exhilaration upon reaching the peak, we can also motivate ourselves with a feeling-charged picture of what things can be like when we are on top of our own life challenges.

A good vision captures how you will feel when you accomplish something.

Often, the first step toward creating or discovering your vision is recognizing that your life is not what it could be. Let these feelings give birth to vision. You can start using this powerful tool to think forward and reshape your future—a future of emotional strength and character.

Creating a vision starts by asking yourself questions like, "Where do I see myself in a week, a month, a year, five years from now? When I look back in five years, and everything I have dreamed about has taken place, what will my life look like?"

Let your imagination run loose. Envision a big picture in your mind, such as creating harmony in your family, developing a great relationship with your wife or changing careers. Then write it in your journal.

When you are finished, write your vision in places where you will see it several times a day. This is not something you need to show others, except perhaps your workout buddies or coach. But keeping a vision before *your* eyes will keep you on track when rough times come.

CREATE A LEGACY

The thoughts, feelings, memories, and the love you leave behind, the kind words you said, the advice you gave, the thoughtful things you have done, the way you touched a life—all of these represent your legacy. What kind of legacy do you want to leave?

The first step toward creating a positive legacy is having a clear vision of the good you want to leave behind. Your character is your legacy. If you were in a business-coaching program, you might also write down the material legacy you would like to leave: the money, the business, the home, the cottage, and so on. You may include these things in your journal, too, but I want you to focus on a vision for your character.

Without a vision, you are unlikely to leave anything worth modeling.

Take the big picture you developed, zoom in, and then focus on the end results of emotional fitness and strong character. See yourself in your mind's eye with the best emotional physique you can develop. See yourself as someone who can finish the race well, lift the weight of responsibility,

160

carry the burden of unselfish love, jump hurdles that block your career, climb sheer rock-face relationship obstacles, and rappel down the other side without flagging. What does vision have to do with leaving a legacy? Everything. Without a vision, you are unlikely to leave anything worth modeling.

Imagine your emotional fitness "before-and-after" photos. Think of magazine pictures showing the chubby guy in his undershirt hiding the roll of fat around his waist in the "before" picture and the "after" shot of the same guy with six-pack abs, biceps flexed, veins popping out as a result of his workout program. What does your emotional "after" shot look like? How do you see yourself living and acting toward others?

Be specific. Have you ever noticed how your dreams motivate you to get up in the morning? Maybe you have dreamed of starting a business or getting a new motorcycle. The more vivid the dream—the more specific the bike model, the engine's horsepower, the decals you see on the side—the more power it has to motivate you.

If creating a vision is a struggle for you, sometimes it helps to reach into the past to envision times when you did the loving thing, the unselfish thing, the time you acted rather than reacted. Take that picture and graft it into the vision of your legacy. Now write down the details of your legacy in your journal. Leave space to add to this vision, because the more vivid and specific it is, the better it will motivate you. Keep adding as your vision grows.

Here is an example of making your vision so specific that it will lead to a lasting legacy:

> *I want cardiovascular strength to go the distance emotionally. I want to endure over the long haul so I can meet the needs of my wife, my children, and my friends. I never want to grow tired of doing good. I want to extend love even when my loved ones disappoint me, upset me or annoy me. I want to exhibit what the Bible calls the Fruit of the Spirit: love, joy, peace, patience, kindness, goodness, faithfulness, gentleness, and self-control.*

Now go ahead and write your own vision!

SET EXERCISE GOALS

If you wanted to run a marathon, lower your golf score substantially or learn how to SCUBA dive, you might see a vision of yourself crossing the finish line, getting a hole in one or swimming among brilliantly colored tropical fish near a coral reef. But if you have never even run a mile, how are you going to finish a marathon? If you seldom play golf, how are you ever going to get out of the sand traps when you do play? And if you cannot swim, well, you might as well forget about SCUBA diving.

To accomplish any goal, you need to break it down into small, measurable segments. If you want to run a marathon, start by running short distances and increasing them gradually. To improve at golf, spend time at the practice range to improve your swing and technique. If you want to SCUBA dive, start by snorkeling.

If you do not break your emotional workout goals into measurable steps, your vision may end up as a grandiose daydream and remain forever beyond your grasp. It is good to stretch and reach for more than you think is possible, but it is not good to lie on the couch expecting the dream to come true because you think you can conjure it into existence by visualizing it hard enough. Visualizing is not a magic spell but a tool to help you find passion, energy, and motivation. You need to be realistic yet flexible with your goals. Do not make them too small and fail to work up a sweat. But do not make them too big and injure yourself either.

READY TO START?

Are you ready to start setting practical and measurable goals? Maybe you have not even started your core or strength exercises. You are skimming through this book and finding it hard to get started, even though you like the ideas and would like to try them. If you have had a difficult time getting started, here is what to do:

- Buy a notebook.
- Write out some emotional exercise goals for the week.

- Be as specific as possible about the time, place, and length of time you are going to spend on each one.
- Make each goal measurable and obtainable.
- Check your progress once a week.

You may also write daily goals, but it is good to have some flexibility in your schedule, and do not let your schedule drive you. Your goals can address all areas of your life: physical, social, family, business, spiritual, financial, emotional, and personal.

Writing down your emotional workout goals on a weekly basis is a foundational endurance exercise in the program. It has been proven that those who write measurable goals are far more likely to succeed and realize their dreams than those who only think about them. People are wired psychologically to live up to their commitments. When you put something in writing, you are committing to it. Merely musing mentally about something or telling yourself you *should* do it is non-committal, and you will not see any results. If you write or draw your overall dream and then write your goals as a way of committing to meet them, you will find yourself with new energy and zest

People are wired psychologically to live up to their commitments.

to meet your targets. There is a psychological force behind commitment that unleashes motivating power. For example, you could write in your journal that you choose to get up at 6:45 a.m.—fifteen minutes before you wife and kids get up—and spend that time quietly reflecting in the B-Zone. Note: I said, "choose." Remember the strengthening exercise of avoiding the words "I should," "I have to" or "I must"?

Use the present tense when setting goals. Write, "I am getting up at 6:45 a.m. every morning." Even if you are not doing it now, you can envision yourself doing that. Write it down, and you will find it that much easier to get out of bed in the morning.

It takes a personal commitment to stay with your plan. If you commit to work out on Monday, Wednesday, and Friday from 7:00 to 8:00 a.m., then make it a priority. It also means that at 8:00, it is time to move on to the rest of the day. If, at 7:30, you realize you are not where you want to be in your workout, it is important to adjust, to change your expectations. Be encouraged that you have moved closer toward accomplishing your goal even if you have not reached it yet.

Make sure your goals are realistic and independent from the performance of others. For example, you may envision having the happiest and healthiest family in your city. Well, your wife and children may block that goal. Your wife may sink into depression. It happens. Despite your best efforts, one of your children might get lured into using drugs or drinking underage. Instead, make it your goal to be the best husband, the father, leader or team player you can be. No matter what anyone else in your life does, they cannot block those goals.

You can control how well you play your position and influence the others on your team to do their best as well. You will find that if you eliminate unrealistic goals involving others, you will be a lot less angry and frustrated. Shift your focus onto yourself and your personal growth, and you will find that by modeling positive change, others close to you will follow.

MEASURE LONG-TERM PROGRESS

Nearly everyone has had the unenviable experience of being micro-managed by a boss. This is not a good feeling. *Why doesn't she trust me? You may have thought. Why is he always looking over my shoulder? Can't she see that I am doing the job?* A good leader understands that employees need clear, specific instructions as well as authority to make decisions that affect their assigned tasks. Once the assignment has been communicated clearly, the leader should step back and observe from a distance without looking over the shoulder or peering at each activity through a micro-scope. Instead, he or she should watch the overall direction and ensure the person has everything he or she needs to do the job and is moving down the path at an appropriate pace. This is called empowerment.

While we long for this sort of treatment from others, how good are we at offering it to ourselves? If we are honest, most of us will admit that we micro-manage ourselves just like the hovering boss. We measure every step of the race, worried that each one is a millimeter too long or too short. We become so pre-occupied with measuring the details of our progress that we lose direction. To help counteract this tendency, use the measurable weekly goals to give you incentive to meet achievable targets, but do not use them to assess your overall growth. Learn to measure your progress over the long-term instead.

Whether it is your physical fitness routine, your golf game or your stock market investments, you have to settle for seeing improvement over the long haul. Prepare yourself: In the short-term, you may see more losers than winners.

When you approach an aggressive physical routine, you get tired. Your muscles ache and seem to go backward in the initial phases. This is normal. Adjustment takes time. So does growing and strengthening. If you are too consumed with measuring short-term gains, emotional fitness routines will seem counterproductive

If you are too consumed with measuring short-term gains, emotional fitness routines will seem counterproductive and counterintuitive.

and counterintuitive. I guarantee that early on, you will find greater struggles, you will feel more tired, your anxiety level will increase, and your ability to cope will fall backward. Again, this is normal. It is merely a function of your greater awareness of how bad things have always been. Do not be consumed, deterred, disillusioned or discouraged with these short-term signs. Focus instead on the big picture of what you want to accomplish.

WRITE AFFIRMATIONS

If you want to add some punch to your goals, try writing affirmations for each one. This is a mini-version of envisioning your legacy. Imagine the result of accomplishing each one in the most positive light you can. Include how you are going to feel. Write it in the present tense as if you have accomplished it already.

For instance, add some zest to your goal of getting up early by saying, "I enjoy waking up in the morning to a silent house and turning my mind to the deepest, most meaningful, and spiritually enriching part of my day. I crave the time to reflect, to read words of truth that feed my soul, to take time to visualize how I want my day to go. I choose to live my life differently from now on."

Try writing your own version, careful to leave out any trace of should or have to, and you will practically bound of bed in the morning. Put the smell of the coffee into your affirmation, the chirp of the birds, whatever it takes to make you look forward to spending that time in your B-Zone workout space.

> *Put the smell of the coffee into your affirmation, the chirp of the birds, whatever it takes to make you look forward to spending that time in your B-Zone workout space.*

For every goal in your life, write a positive affirmation that says, in effect, "I can do this, and I feel terrific when I do." Envision yourself accomplishing that goal. You can use these affirmations in your strength training to replace the negative thoughts you need to resist, such as: *This will never work. I'm a failure. Forget about it; It's not worth it.*

The more consistently you practice endurance exercises by keeping your legacy in mind, setting practical, measurable written goals, and writing affirmations, the more you will find

166

yourself motivated to accomplish those goals and move toward making your legacy real.

DISCOVER YOUR PASSION

A key endurance exercise involves discovering your passion. Have you ever thought about what this might be? Get out your notebook and answer the following questions. What drives you? What makes you want to get out of bed in the morning? Reflect on the times that you have been happiest in your life. What were you doing? If money were no object, what would you do with your time? What sort of work would you do? What could you do twenty-four hours a day and never get tired of doing it?

Sometimes living out your passion requires a spiritual and emotional journey to find the courage and strength to follow your inmost desires.

If you do not know yet what your passion is, it is time to discover it. If you have no idea, start with a process of elimination. What do you dislike? As you list what you do not like, what you passionately desire may become clear in contrast. Use your Being Zone time to reflect on who you are and what gives you the deepest sense of satisfaction.

Once you discover your passion, you may find that your job, your business, even your hobbies are not in sync with it. Sometimes living out your passion requires a spiritual and emotional journey to find the courage and strength to follow your inmost desires.

Eagle's Flight, the corporate training outfit I helped to build, was not my passion, even though the work interested and excited me. With enough focus, commitment, and diligence, I could have continued my work there, but it was not fulfilling. When I left, I wanted the second half of my life to align with my passion.

167

It took three years of deep reflection and daily emotional workouts to fully understand and realize that my passion is to help people accomplish what is possible in their personal lives, to help individuals reach their full potential wherever they find themselves, not only in the business setting. If you find one or two points in this book that change your life for the better, then discovering my passion will have been worth it.

Take time to develop your vision, then ask yourself: *Does it fall in line with my passion?* The more your passion is incorporated into your vision, the more motivated you will be to achieve it.

EXAMINE YOUR PRINCIPLES

Make sure your principles refine and support your passion. Principles are timeless truths that govern your life. They have to do with integrity, honesty, and respect, treating others the way you want to be treated. Let them guide the choices you make.

Have you examined your moral principles lately? They form the ground on which you stand. How steadily have you planted your feet before you lift the weight of your passion? Are you standing on something solid or is the ground crumbling under your feet?

One principle is to build self-esteem by doing something worthy of esteem. If you lie, cheat, and steal, it is unlikely that you will feel good about yourself. Think about your principles. How firm are they? Can you be bought? Know where you would draw a line in the sand and take a stand. As you examine your principles and reflect on your behavior, you will find many areas where you fall short. Resist the temptation to define yourself by your failures. Instead, choose to live differently from now on.

KNOW YOUR MISSION

Do you know what your mission in life is? If you are in business for yourself or managing a team, you may have crafted a mission statement. A mission is all about your purpose—why you believe you exist. Only you have the ability to identify and carry out the unique purpose for your life.

> *Do you know what your mission in life is?*

Try to write a mission statement for your personal life in a sentence or two. Your life's mission is closely related to your legacy, your vision, your passion, and whom you desire to serve. My mission is to serve men who want to become strong husbands, fathers, and leaders—to help them become more emotionally and spiritually fit. See how my mission lines up with my passion and how it focuses on whom I desire to serve? Now try writing yours.

ADJUST YOUR FOCUS

As you grow emotionally, your dreams and goals will change. New vistas will open up. You will see new mountains you want to climb and new areas of strength to develop. The fresher and more vivid your dreams, the more consistently you will commit yourself—in writing—to meeting smaller targets and measurable goals. The harder you work at achieving them, the sooner your dreams will come true. Keep your dreams, goals, and vision fluid. You will draw vitality from your successes and look forward to the challenge of new horizons.

OVERCOME OBSTACLES

Obstacles to your passion, mission, and vision are bound to come. Good strategic planning identifies not only the appropriate goals but also predicts the potential obstacles and how to address them before they appear. Obstacles are normal and frequent. The road to emotional fitness is riddled with them. Overcoming each one is what the race is all about. We all face difficulties in our lives. Instead of perceiving them as problems and setbacks, see them as opportunities to grow. See yourself as running an obstacle race. The bigger the obstacle over which you can sail, the better athlete you are.

TAKE TIME OUT

Sometimes the game of life happens too fast for us, and we cannot stay on top. Our actions and words hurt others, especially those who are on our side. It is far better to be up front and call a time-out—giving the other person time and space away from us—than to keep them close. During these time-outs, we need to reflect on what is going wrong and make adjustments. An apology, taking responsibility, putting someone else's needs ahead of ours are all positive adjustments.

No one is perfect. We all make mistakes. However, those who do not learn from their mistakes are more likely to repeat them, thus causing them to be demoted to the minors or released from their contracts. These people may be headed for divorce, alienation from their kids, being bypassed for a promotion or getting fired from a job.

No one likes to be cut from the team, but sometimes, tough love demands severe consequences.

You may also have to call a time-out from someone in your life who is behaving abusively or irresponsibly. No one likes to be cut from the team, but sometimes, tough love demands severe consequences. This is not something negative. It just means you are willing to take control of your life and take care of yourself.

SAMPLE ENDURANCE WORKOUT

When sitting down to do my endurance workout for the week, I review my legacy, my vision, my passion, and my mission. Next, I look at my game plan, my overall goals—short-term and long-term—and the accompanying affirmations. I adjust them, add to them, and see whether or not I am on target.

After crafting your vision or legacy, you can start with small goals that lead to the bigger picture. You can incorporate something that can be accomplished on a daily or weekly basis. For example, you sit down with your journal on a Sunday and write that you want to spend less time in the D-Zone during the next week. You also want to get out of the C-Zone in less time than it takes you normally. Now, to make these goals measurable and to develop a strategy using the various workouts in this book, write down the when, where, how much, and how long for each exercise you choose for the week.

Use the Zone check-up as a core exercise several times a day. This will give you a record of how much time you usually spend in zones D or C, allowing you to make a meaningful comparison. Here is what an endurance workout might look like:

1. Perform a Zone check-up at 6:50 a.m., 12:00 noon, and 10:00 p.m. each day and record the results.

2. Set aside fifteen minutes of B-Zone time from 6:45 until 7:00 every morning from Monday to Friday. On Saturdays and Sundays, schedule it at 7:30 a.m. (Remember that many of the exercises you do are preventive exercises. If you enter the B-Zone faithfully, you will go into zones D and C far less often, because you will not react like a puppet to your circumstances. You will be more proactive.)

3. In addition to the Zone check-up, write ten things for which you are grateful while reflecting in the B-Zone. Read your vision and mission statements. Spend five minutes praying. (You can choose which strength, endurance, and core exercises you will include. For example, you can do one exercise three times a week instead of every day. You can do a relationship inventory every six months.)

4. If you discover you are in the D-Zone, take time out to reflect and to observe your anger and frustration instead of inflicting it on someone else. Add another ten minutes to your reflection time, either on the spot

or during your lunch hour. Check five (or ten—you choose the number) times a day to make sure you are not judging, blaming or holding a grudge. Step up your efforts to resist negative thoughts and replace them with positive truths.

5. If you find that you are in the C-Zone, take time to reflect on your anxiety, fear, and self-condemnation. Check often to make sure you are resisting negative thoughts and replacing them with "I can" statements and affirmations.

6. Set aside two hours one weekday evening to read a book that helps you develop better communication, anger management or anxiety-reduction strategies.

7. Attend a men's group meeting and call one of your workout buddies to have coffee for mutual encouragement.

HEAD FORWARD

When we train in earnest, we have to break bad habits we have picked up over the years. For example, many people think that, when running, you should put the heel down first. But endurance runners know to place the mid-sole of the foot down first and take shorter steps. This forces the body forward and places the head in front of the feet. This produces a sensation of falling forward and the feet are trying to catch up to keep you from landing on your face. Although it is important to lean forward into every step, it is more important to lean forward into the overall direction you are going.

Chris Munford gave me a football analogy for this principle: He described how the defensive back spends a lot of time running backward, trying to anticipate where the other team's receiver is going to go. As soon as someone on the opposite team throws the ball, the defensive back has to change direction and beat the receiver to the ball. Chris calls that moment the critical "break point."

One of the techniques a defensive back uses to change direction so quickly is to "pop" his head in the direction he wants to go. "The head is a heavy 'appendage,' so to speak," Chris say, "and turning one's head and throwing it in the direction one wants to go propels the rest of the body forward in the direction of the receiver and the thrown ball. At the professional level, where everybody is fast, defensive backs who can effectively pop their heads and use them as a sort of directional ballast are the ones who are most successful."

Think of this when you are working on emotional endurance. It is critical to put your head first—to be forward thinking, to be leaning in the direction you want to go and believing the rest of you will catch up. This is the "endurance posture" for the times when you are tired and would rather slow down. Remaining in that forward, *believing* posture allows you to break through into a stronger and more lasting second wind. So lean into it. Capture the exhilaration. Train yourself in the emotional marathon. You are in the race. You have a number on your chest. Do not stand on the sidelines cheering other runners on, hoping you might be out there some day. It is time for you to join in. Contrary to what you may have been taught, everyone is designed for this race. It is ours to run and ours to finish well.

It is critical to put your head first—to be forward thinking, to be leaning in the direction you want to go and believing the rest of you will catch up.

CHAPTER 12:

COPING WITH INJURY

When exercising to the point of positive failure, there will be normal pain. Muscles that you have not used in a while will cry out. Lactic acid in the fibers will create a dull ache that increased circulation will carry away.

But injury is a different matter. It usually results from doing an exercise the wrong way, attempting it with too much weight or starting without a proper warm-up. If you injure yourself, recovery takes precious time that could have been used for strengthening.

Trying to do it alone and ignoring your emotional workout routines will set others and yourself up for injury. When emotionally injured or injuring others, you become a liability for your team. Once injured, it becomes more difficult to open up, to trust, and to communicate freely. You may already be injured from past trauma before you even start to work out.

When exercising, it is helpful to work similar muscles from different positions. This takes your mind off the exercise's difficulty and allows you to push through to greater strength, endurance, and results. On a stationary bicycle, for example, putting your hands above your head and closing

Once injured, it becomes more difficult to open up, to trust, and to communicate freely.

175

your eyes can take your focus off the burning in your legs and allow you to push harder.

Consider how this principle can influence your emotional exercise. Going for a long walk with a workout buddy or exploring different coffee shops can be enough of a diversion to allow you to work through a struggle. Invite your wife out to dinner to have the discussion you have been dreading. Changing the surroundings in which a crisis normally occurs allows you to push harder to reach honest dialogue and understanding.

Sprinters have a longer recovery time than marathon runners. They have to push themselves to the maximum of their capability, to their absolute limit three or four times in the heats of the competition. While I am sure sprinters have their unique challenges, marathon runners have the ability to pace themselves over the long haul. Sprinting is hard on the nervous system. When we hit an emotional blowout or crisis, we max out. Like the sprinter, expect a longer recovery time. The better shape you are in, the shorter your recovery time will be. The following exercises can help you to decrease your recovery time and speed healing of past injuries. Working on these regularly with your workout buddy, coach, or group will enable you to deal with crises more effectively and allow your system to recover faster, ensuring that you get back in the game.

IDENTIFY THE EXTENT OF YOUR INJURY

In your B-Zone time or while you are journaling, be gut-level honest. Denial will keep you in emotional pain. Do not be afraid to seek professional help if needed. For instance, if you have experienced abuse as a child, you may need people with more knowledge and experience than what your workout buddies or coach can offer.

COMPENSATE FOR YOUR INJURY
WHILE TRAINING

Someone with a strained rotator cuff cannot lift his arm above his head without considerable shoulder pain. In the same way, those who have

176

gone through emotional injury cannot be expected to deal with certain circumstances without facing excruciating pain. To work through muscle and tendon injury, exercise is critical. However, it is just as important to ensure that the form, duration, and intensity of the workout are appropriate for strengthening the weakened muscles. Train yourself to isolate and then strengthen the injured and weakened emotional muscles. To avoid further injury, you may need to exercise muscles you did not know you had. An emotional parallel would be avoiding a person who has hurt you in the past while talking through your feelings and actions with your coach or workout buddies.

PRACTICE ROLE-PLAYING

This is another good way to work out an emotional injury. Have your coach or buddy act as the person who damaged you. Use role-playing to express how you feel. This is a great idea if the person who injured you is no longer alive or if he or she would fire you if you aired your grievances. Continue working through your injury until it no longer controls you emotionally.

CHAPTER 13

ADVANCED WORKOUT

I n any workout program, it is advisable to start small and build gradually. Once you are stronger, you add new weights, new skills, and new challenges. It is the same with your emotional workout. I advise you not to start using these techniques in this chapter right away but to build your emotional physique with the core, strength, and endurance exercises first. Find some workout buddies. Meet on a regular basis. Once you are used to the process, you can try some of these advanced techniques.

ACCOUNTABILITY

In earlier chapters, I spoke about being accountable to others. Accountability does not just happen unless you make a big mistake others can see. Most of the time, your friends might not know whether something is wrong. We have learned to hide our emotional lives. If you want someone to hold you accountable, you must open yourself up to scrutiny. You need to share your goals, your successes, and your failures. Seek to be accountable in meetings with your workout buddies or take one trusted member of the group aside for a cup of coffee and set up an accountability agenda.

Here is what to do:

- Disclose your emotional workout goals.
- Reveal your failures and successes.
- Be honest! Do not minimize or maximize your faults or your accomplishments.
- Give the group or partner permission to give you feedback on what you have said.
- Listen to observations and advice. Take what applies to you and discard the rest.
- Ask appropriate questions to ensure each of you is on track.
- Restate your commitments.

Are you in an accountability relationship? If not, are you ready to begin one?

TRI-ACCOUNTABILITY

For my coaching program, I have developed a system for tri-accountability that mirrors tri-training: core, strength, and endurance. This is a more formal set-up for accountability and involves a minimum of three people who have each agreed to take responsibility for one of the areas. Having an accountability group of at least three people will help in a variety of ways. For one, it will be more balanced. Just as a three-legged stool never rocks, meeting with three people is a stable platform. Tri-accountability provides a healthy diversity of opinion and critical insights that may not occur in a twosome. Second, if one person cannot make the meeting (this will be a rare exception, because these meetings are a high priority), it can still go on.

Here is how you can set up tri-accountability:

1. Think through the commitment involved. Anticipate obstacles and adjust accordingly. Can you deliver? Be clear on your expectations. Ask yourself and the others what is needed, by when, and how?

180

2. Have an up-front agreement. Give each other permission to speak honestly. There is nothing more obnoxious than someone who points out other people's faults without being invited to do so.

3. Agree to meet on a regular basis. Pin down a consistent time each week so you are not always juggling your schedule. If you mutually agree to do certain workouts in between meetings, do them in advance of the deadline.

4. Assign a captain to each tri-training area: core, strength, and endurance. This will help each member become comfortable with asking different kinds of accountability questions, all of which are important. Change roles until everyone is familiar with and can understand how each type of question applies. Soon, you will find that your ability to ask these questions of yourself and others will become natural. You can use the exercises in this book to form the basis for accountability questions on each area. Here are some sample questions for each of your tri-accountability leaders.

CORE QUESTIONS

- In what ways did you stretch yourself emotionally this week?
- How centered and balanced has the week been?
- How much time did you set aside in the *Being Zone* each day?
- How are your Zone check-ups going?
- What sort of helpful books have you been reading? What have you learned?
- How often have you been writing in your journal?
- What sort of important realizations did you make this week?
- Did you hit positive failure in any area this week? Describe the experience.

- How much time did you take to pray this week?
- Are you working and living out of what's important to you, or has something else come in and taken priority? Is this really a priority or a priority imposter?
- Are you getting off-balance on any issue?
- What does your relationship inventory look like for the past week?
- What does your calendar inventory tell you about your week?
- How much time did you arrange to spend alone this week?
- How much time did you spend practicing your listening skills?
- For what are you most thankful this week?
- Have you been looking after your health? Exercising? Eating right? Getting enough sleep?

STRENGTH QUESTIONS

- How long can you resist your anger? Did you grow in this ability this week?
- How successful have you been in responding in a reasonable, measured way to provocation instead of reacting angrily?
- Can you give an example of how have you resisted judging?
- How successfully have you resisted self-condemnation?
- How effective are you at stopping yourself from blaming others or making excuses for yourself?
- Any burnout sets this week? Could you push through and keep working out?
- How successful have you been at replacing negative feelings with an attitude of gratitude?
- How are you doing at forgiving on the spot? Is there anyone you need to forgive?
- What negative thoughts and feelings have you noticed this week? How did you deal with them?
- When you replaced negative thoughts with positive ones, did you notice any change in how you felt?

- Have you separated people from problems successfully over the past week?
- Have you resisted the desire to control other people and events?
- Does anyone you know deserve an apology from you? Did you find the strength to make a genuine apology?
- What new communication exercises did you practice this week? How did they work?
- Did you ask for help this week when needed?
- What efforts have you taken to make new friends?
- How well did you manage your calendar this week? Did you drive it or did you allow it to drive you?
- How successful were you at eliminating "I should" or "I have to" from your vocabulary?
- How did you go out of your way to serve someone who needs help this week?

ENDURANCE QUESTIONS

- How much time did you take to set goals and affirmations for the week?
- What legacy do you want to leave?
- What would you like your life to look like in five years? Ten years?
- What does your emotional fitness "after" shot look like? How much do you resemble that image right now?
- What is your mission statement? Have you altered it in any way this week?
- How has what you did this week been in line with your mission statement?
- Have you examined your principles? What have you done to live up to them?
- Did you learn anything about your passion this week? How have you acted out of your passion this week?
- What were your short-term goals for the past week? Did you write down your goals? Did you achieve them?

- What are your emotional workout goals for next week?
- How are your short-term goals taking your toward your finish line?
- What sort of affirmations have you written to go with your goals?
- What are you doing to stay on track?
- How has writing your goals helped you this week?
- What skills do you need to develop to help you reach your goals?
- What obstacles did you face this week? How did you overcome them?
- Did you have to call any time-outs? How many? Why did you have to call them?
- How well did you do at "forward thinking"?

TRI-ACCOUNTABILITY FORM

You have my permission to make a copy of the following form to establish your contact information and assignments for core, strength, and endurance if you enter into tri-accountability.

Date: _____

This sheet will become an agreement of accountability among the following three people.

Name: 1: _____ 2: _____ 3: _____

**Initial
Responsibility:**   Core   Strength   Endurance

Contact: Phone: _____ Phone: _____ Phone: _____
                 E-mail: _____ E-mail: _____ E-mail: _____

Lead Contact:
We have agreed that _____will have the responsibility of lead contact. This individual will be responsible to ensure that the meeting times and dates are communicated clearly to the others.

We will meet _____(how often), to encourage each other to reach our goals.

Meeting Date(s): _____
Time: _____

Signed:

_____

_____

_____

COACH OTHERS

As you build your emotional muscles, you will reach a point where you can start to lift up your brothers. Once you become stronger, it is your turn to pass along what you have learned about emotional fitness training. It is time for you to model the right way to behave in the *Actualizing Zone*.

When someone looks up to you and follows your example, you will be even more motivated to maintain your own workout program. Cultivate whatever you are asking the other person to aspire to. This is a journey; so do not expect perfection from yourself or the one you are coaching. Model the life of a man who is serious about getting stronger, but make sure the other person does not become overly dependent on you. You will have to learn how to set him on his feet without knocking him off balance. This takes patience as you help him grow without demanding more than he can give.

CENTER YOURSELF IN PRAYER

Can you be alone without some sort of diversion? Seventeenth-century mathematician and philosopher Blaise Pascal wrote in his classic work *Pensées*, "I have discovered that all the unhappiness of men arises from one single fact that they cannot stay quietly in their own chamber."[3]

In one of the core exercises, I recommended that you wake up early to reflect—to give yourself a tune-up for the day. In this advanced version, you will try to sit still and reflect without reading or without an agenda. Just sit and wait. Set a time limit, maybe five or ten minutes at first.

Your first time might bore you so bad that you will literally count the seconds, waiting impatiently for your quiet time to end. You might feel like running out of the room screaming at the top of your lungs. Or you might fall asleep. I suggest that you set a timer and make yourself sit alone for set amount of time. Start small and build. Discipline yourself to sit still, even when you hit a wall of anxiety. Extreme boredom that makes you feel twitchy is the first sign you are hitting the wall. Then you might encounter anxiety that makes you feel as if you are going nuts. If you sit and wait through this, you will make some amazing personal discoveries after this anxiety fades. And it will fade.

In physical training, I hated some of the core exercises Chris had me do; but I saw the benefits over time, so I persisted. It is the same with tough disciplines like sitting still without distractions. You will find the results showing after you pass through the wall of positive failure—the place where you push through the boredom and anxiety—to see what is behind it. You will gain insight that is scary at first, but keep at it, because you will grow stronger and change for the better, from the inside out.

Your goal is to really hear what is going on inside yourself, not to blank out your mind or suspend your will or judgment.

I call this exercise *centering prayer*. In religious circles, it is referred to as "practicing the presence of God" or meditation. The key is to stay present in the moment—be aware of yourself, your body, your thoughts, and your surroundings.

Your goal is to really *hear* what is going on inside yourself, not to blank out your mind or suspend your will or judgment. If you sit alone in a room, it is easy for your thoughts and imagination to drift. You can get carried away thinking about what you are going to say to your boss, your wife, yours kids or whoever upset you last. Ever notice how you can forget about your surroundings when you are caught up in some rehearsed conversation or daydream? You could spend hours dreaming about the boat that you want to buy or some other toy. These are distractions, too.

If you are going to spend time alone in a place where the phone or family members will not interrupt you, try to remain aware of your physical surroundings, even though your eyes might be closed. Stay in the present moment and observe your thoughts rather than allowing them to carry you away. When your thoughts come, question them. Ask yourself, "Why do I feel this way? What is causing my anxiety, worry or fear?" When you get past the surface stuff, you will begin to understand what is driving your behavior.

You will be amazed at what you learn about your thought life and feelings. Through this practice, you will discover things about yourself that others may see but that you have blocked from view because you have been running away. You may discover anger, hurt, and anxiety that you never realized were there.

The best times to journal are at the beginning or the end of each day.

This exercise works best when practiced in a disciplined fashion over time. The insights and awareness may not come during the sessions themselves. In fact, you may feel uncomfortable during centering prayer and find it nearly impossible to discipline your thoughts and remain present and aware in the moment. If so, you have not failed. The discomfort is a sign of how hard you are working. The benefits will come after you start going about your day—benefits such as a sense of peace or thought-provoking insights.

Even if your centering prayer becomes difficult and dry, if you practice regularly, you will feel calmer, more aware, and more balanced in the same way that a good physical workout will leave you feeling energized, alert, and connected to your body. You may want to try doing this centering exercise in the morning before you start the day and/or in the evening before you go to bed.

ADVANCED JOURNALING

If you have been using a notebook for writing your goals each week and keeping a record of your emotional workouts, you have already begun to journal. Here are some advanced journaling techniques that may feel as risky as backcountry snowboarding or as awkward as the first time sparring in karate class. But risks like these can be exhilarating.

As you build a habit of reflective time, start recording your thoughts, impressions, growing edge, and moments of positive failure. If you have a vivid or meaningful dream, write it down when you wake up. You may have more interesting dreams after you start working out your emotions. Write down your insights, intentions, feelings, desires, issues, challenges, ideals, learning, quotations, and ideas.

The best times to journal are at the beginning or the end of each day. Find a quiet space and reflect on the day's events. Feel free to journal at other times when you are inspired or need to capture something that you can reflect on later.

When you start this free-form style of journaling for the first time, you may not know what to do. Here are some suggestions:

- **Start writing:** Sometimes it helps to start by writing whatever comes to mind—whatever you are thinking about. Give yourself five or ten minutes. The first words may seem strange. Or you might find you are writing lists of things you have to do. Keep writing. As soon as you are able, move into reflecting about yourself.
- **Successes and failures:** Make a list of your successes and failures that day or the day before. Reflect on why you failed or succeeded. What might you have done differently? Write it down. If you write journal entries immediately after a difficult confrontation, then, later on when you are calmer, you can read your entry and reflect on how you could have done things differently. It can be encouraging to look over entries from a year or two ago to observe your progress.
- **Emotions:** Describe how you feel and why.
- **Personal discoveries:** Write what you are discovering about yourself and others.
- **Challenges:** List the challenges you face. Which ones are internal? Which are external?
- **Major accomplishments:** Do not forget to journal regularly about positive things in your life, including the milestones you have reached in moving toward your goals.

189

- **Memories:** You may find long-buried memories surfacing during your reflection time. Capture them in your journal.
- **Patterns:** You may discover patterns of behavior, patterns in your relationships, or patterns in how you communicate. Write down what you observe.
- **Drawings:** Drawing an image or sketch sometimes captures your feelings and realizations better than words. Sometimes you will capture underlying connections and relationships with a diagram.
- **Ask questions:** Use your journal to pose questions to yourself that you do not ask normally. What do I want? Where am I now? Do I have a clear sight on my goals or has my vision become clouded? What would be a perfect day for me? What causes me to give up? Where do I see growth in my life? What do I find particularly challenging? Take a moment to reflect on each one then write down your answers.
- **Prayers:** Write out your prayers or those you find in other books that inspire you.
- **First thoughts in the morning:** What did you wake up thinking about this morning? This is a good way to discover what is uppermost in your mind.
- **Special learning:** If you have discovered something new, write it down.
- **Poems:** If you feel moved to write a poem, put it in your journal. Copy a poem that you love.
- **Musings:** Use your journal to brainstorm. Muse, ponder, and play with ideas without allowing thoughts like "It will never work" or "This is stupid" to stop you.
- **Experiences:** Something happens at work that throws you into positive failure. Your child does something astonishing. You find yourself behaving in a new way that surprises and pleases you. These are all examples of experiences. Write them down.
- **Holiday reflections:** Set aside time to reflect on how you are spending your holidays and what they mean to you. Write down your memories of holidays past.

Here is an example from my journal to show how I used some regular exercises and advanced techniques in my *Being Zone* workout space.

A JOURNAL ENTRY: OUT OF WHACK

June 20, 2003

Slept in. Started the day dealing with a few things that threw me out of whack. I'm feeling a strong pull to go into the D-Zone or the C-Zone. It doesn't matter which one I enter, when I get there I know I'll have to self-correct and move out. So I am struggling to get into B by making an entry in my journal.

I completed a Zone check-up. On that day, I was not doing so hot! Then I began to reflect on how my past behavior had affected my wife.

Because of my past anger and destructive nature, when Cathy has to disclose things to me, she positions herself to ensure that I'm ready to hear something by saying things like, "I'm about to say something that could upset you" or "I need to tell you something, but I haven't until now because I've been worried about how you will take it. Please do not get angry." Or she'll say, "I've been waiting for the right time to say this, because I know how you might respond."

While I agree with the intent of these precursor statements, they have a tendency to rile me. I hear, "You get angry. I'm scared of your anger. The way you respond to my mistakes is not appropriate." It seems to throw off the balance of the issue, like it is my anger that is the issue, not what she wants to disclose.

If Cathy were to state the ownership of her issue, it might help me see a balanced equation: "Honey, I love you and I'm approaching you softly, but I made a mistake that you need to know about. I waited 'til now to tell you, because it may have been more difficult for you to hear yesterday. Please do not get angry."

The request "please do not get angry" at this point would be redundant because I'd feel as if I'm being approached as kind-hearted instead of tyrannical.

Let's take a look at what I wrote in my journal. I blamed my wife again. I am not the first one to do this. Most of us know about the Garden of Eden and what happened there. The serpent tempted Eve; she ate the apple and then gave it to Adam. When God asked Adam why he ate it, Adam blamed Eve. Men have been playing the same game in their marriages ever since.

Recording these thoughts allowed me to acknowledge my anger, honestly observe my thoughts, and examine the cause for my upset. Merely by recording what I thought and felt, I began to move into the *Being Zone*. That is where my reflection took me.

Unfortunately, tyrannical is what I deserve, because that is the track I have worn down consistently over many years, and to undo this I need to show higher character consistently and help to fill in the groove or crevasse with evidence of that change in me whenever it appears in Cathy. It is my duty. It is my role. I need to own my part of what's been created in her. I also need to roll up my sleeves and help smooth out this issue for her, because she is my wife, my confidante, and my very best friend.

In the above paragraph, I moved over the C-Zone to get into the B-Zone. Remember the sand trap analogy? Just as blaming Cathy is a D-Zone trait, blaming myself lands me in the C-Zone if I dwell on my mistakes and beat myself up for them. Yes, I needed to acknowledge my role in making Cathy tiptoe around me. But I must not fall into the sand trap of self-loathing or self-condemnation, no matter how unflattering my realizations are.

So here in the B-Zone it becomes clear: To live in the A-Zone, I need to build positively into Cathy a new legacy and help her come to terms with her fear of failure or embarrassment, a fear that I have helped create.

I want to stay out of the C-Zone, resist blaming myself for my current state, and stay hopeful and proactive.

I must also heed her wonderful advice: "Do not let this move you into the D-Zone, honey. I need you in the A-Zone. I need you."

I can do that. I will do that.

CHAPTER 14:

STAY IN THE GAME

THE SMELL OF SWEAT

When I was four years old, my parents took me to visit my missionary grandparents in Africa. I spent the summer there, discovering a whole new world of grass huts, crocodiles, and fresh mangos hanging from low branches. We traveled dusty, two-track roads in the back of my grandfather's Land Rover.

I remember the church services on those hot, dry days, the pungent aroma of many bodies packed together on crude wooden benches in a grass-roofed building. Since then, entering a gym after a basketball game or a locker room after a sports event brings me back to that time as a child. It triggers something deep inside, bringing back a flood of feelings.

Your changed life is the best statement you can make.

Have you ever felt emotions hanging heavy in the air, making the atmosphere thick and rank like the smell of sweat? My house does not smell like a gym, but sometimes when entering the front door after a day's work, I sense thick emotions. I just know something has been going on. Perhaps my kids have been fighting or my wife is discouraged or frustrated. Nothing needs to be said. You know what I am talking about. You can feel it.

You have a choice to make when you confront the "smell of sweat" in your home. I find that sometimes a mechanism kicks in saying, "Whoa! Do I want to confront what's been happening here? Do I want a part of this? Maybe I should go back to work or find some other way to duck out. Do I really want to ask, 'How was your day?'" This is when you have to make a conscious decision to put your workouts into practice, to use the muscles you have developed already . I hope you are strong enough. If not, do the best you can, but do not exceed your limits. If you bow out without trying, you will miss an opportunity to listen, to empathize, and to connect. Bowing out, you are likely to grow more distant from the ones you love.

As Dr. Richard Carlson says in his best-selling series, "don't sweat the small stuff," such as when your wife disagrees with your opinion now and then. It is easier to face these minor issues when you are in shape. You will develop a greater sensitivity to the emotional currents around you that you were either oblivious to or avoided facing. Grab the rope in the great relationship tug-of-war. Be there for your wife and kids. You will never regret rising to the challenge, and they will thank you for it.

BALANCE YOUR EMOTIONAL "DIET"

As part of your centering exercises, you need to pay attention to your emotional diet—what you are feeding your mind and soul. This is related to your relationship and time inventories. It includes the books you read, the television you watch, the games you play on the computer, and the movies you rent.

If you have been doing the reflective, centering exercises in the Core Training chapter and the resistance exercises in the Developing Strength chapter, you know from experience how your thoughts and feelings influence each other. If you can change your thinking about an issue, it will affect your feelings and could result in a new game plan. Changing your thinking is challenging. It takes perseverance and time.

But, like any change, it is possible with the appropriate equipment, focus, and perseverance. This means you change your thinking when being bombarded by negative images, thoughts, and ideas.

Even if you are carving out time to read enlightening books and doing the exercises, are you still holding onto a corner of your life where you allow negative influences to infect you? Think about the places you visit, the Internet sites you surf when no one is around. Remember the saying: Garbage in, garbage out.

LOSE THE MUSCLE SHIRT

Don't you hate it when some guy you know starts working out, builds his pecs and biceps, then swaggers around in a muscle shirt, bragging about his exercise regimen and prodding you to lose weight? Make sure you do not do the same thing now that you are working out emotionally. Once you start seeing positive results, you will be tempted to talk about your workout with everyone you meet. You will begin to notice the dumb, competitive conversations. You will become increasingly aware of how many men are running away from their responsibilities into mindless diversion. Have some compassion. Remember that not long ago, you were one of those guys yourself. Do not be too hard on them. There is no need to show off.

Instead, lose the muscle shirt and show how fit you are through your actions. Look for opportunities to influence others without coming across as better than they are. Do not give unwanted advice. Not everyone is as interested in your workout as you are. When others see how well you are playing your position, they will ask you how you do it. They will want what you have. Then you can share your workout secrets.

And when they do ask, invite them to join your workout group. Give them a copy of this book. But remember: Your changed life is the best statement you can make.

THE EMOTIONAL MIRROR SURVEY[4]

"WHAT I SEE"

Date: _____

Survey Instructions:

When you fill out this survey, reflect on how you usually think or behave. Do not labor over the questions. Your gut-level answer is usually the best one. If you do not spend any longer than thirty seconds per question, it will take you no more than twenty minutes to fill out. When answering, please use the following scale:

0=Never	**1=Seldom**	**2=Sometimes,**
3=Often	**4=Most times**	**5=Always**

1. __ I am looking for clarity about my next step in life.
2. __ I am making progress toward specific goals in my life.
3. __ I find comfort in pointing out the faults of others.
4. __ I behave in a way that is consistent with my principles.
5. __ I am very quick to protect my possessions.
6. __ I believe the world is basically an unfriendly place.
7. __ I am tender with those I love.
8. __ I do not understand why people cannot see the world as I do.
9. __ I ask many people for their opinions about what I am doing.
10. __ I believe that overall, I am very productive. I get a lot done.
11. __ I tell people what I think about something right out—whether they want to hear it or not.
12. __ I replay conversations and events, wishing I could change what I said or did.

13. __ I am more likely to get angry than choked up about things.
14. __ My philosophy is: "If you get along with me, I get along with you."
15. __ I know my priorities and keep them straight.
16. __ I know there are things I could improve about myself, and I am working on them.
17. __ I admit that sometimes I seek out confrontation.
18. __ I spend more time planning and thinking than actually doing.
19. __ I have some bad habits, habits I know I should change.
20. __ I enjoy spending time with ideas—thinking, talking or reading.
21. __ I am likely to call or write someone after a conversation and clarify what I meant.
22. __ I do not make judgments on how others live but focus on living the best life I can.
23. __ I do not express a lot of tender emotions with the ones I love.
24. __ I do not look for confrontation, but I can defend my position strongly if needed.
25. __ I feel good about where I am right now.
26. __ I am more of a pessimist than an optimist.
27. __ Self-development is a major priority for me.
28. __ I find feedback and criticism difficult to take.
29. __ People close to me say I am moody.
30. __ I often dismiss feelings or opinions that differ from my own.
31. __ I have no trouble standing up for what I believe.
32. __ I appreciate people's honest feedback about me.
33. __ I often find that I magnify problems.
34. __ I am looking for coaching and mentoring.
35. __ I am in the midst of a life change right now.
36. __ I ask a lot of those who love me.
37. __ I do not look for feedback from others. What I think matters most.
38. __ I believe there are many ways to look at any situation.
39. __ I believe if I do not look out for myself, no one else will.
40. __ I tend to open up about my past and myself too early in a relationship.

"WHAT OTHERS SEE"

Dear _____,

I have discovered a helpful book called *Sweating From Your Eyes: Emotional Fitness for Men* by Dave Loney. It is going to help me make a difference in my life and the lives of those around me.

As part of this process, I would like you to fill out the following survey for me, please. It should take no more than twenty minutes. It will help me see myself as others see me. When you consider the answers, reflect on how you see me—how I come across normally to you. Do not worry about telling me something I do not want to hear. The goal of this exercise is not self-affirmation but an accurate reflection of my emotional well being.

Thank you for doing this. I appreciate it.

Sincerely,

_____.

"WHAT OTHERS SEE"

Date: _____

Filled out by: _____

Regarding: _____

Survey Instructions:

Do not labor over the questions. Your gut-level answer is usually the best one. When answering, please use the following scale:

0=Never   **1=Seldom**   **2=Sometimes**
3=Often   **4=Most times**   **5=Always**

1. ___ He is looking for clarity about his next step in life.
2. ___ He is making progress toward specific goals in his life.
3. ___ He finds comfort in pointing out the faults of others.
4. ___ He behaves in a way that is consistent with his principles.
5. ___ He is quick to protect his possessions.
6. ___ He believes the world is basically an unfriendly place.
7. ___ He is tender with those he loves.
8. ___ He does not understand how people cannot see the world as he does.
9. ___ He asks many people for their opinions about what he is doing.
10. ___ He is very productive. He gets a lot done.
11. ___ He tells people what he thinks about something right out— whether they want to hear it or not.
12. ___ He replays conversations and events, wishing he could change what he said or did.
13. ___ He is much more likely to get angry than choked up about things.
14. ___ His philosophy is, "If you get along with me, I get along with you."
15. ___ He knows his priorities and keeps them straight.
16. ___ He knows there are things he could improve about himself, and he is working on them.

17. __ Sometimes, he seeks out confrontation.
18. __ He spends more time planning and thinking than actually doing.
19. __ He has some habits that are bad for him that he knows he should change.
20. __ He enjoys spending a lot of time with ideas—thinking, talking or reading.
21. __ He is likely to call or write someone after a conversation and clarify what he meant.
22. __ He does not make judgments on how others live but focuses on living the best life he can.
23. __ His is not one to express a lot of tender emotions with the people he loves.
24. __ He does not look for confrontation but can defend his position strongly if needed.
25. __ He feels good about where he is right now.
26. __ He is more of a pessimist than an optimist.
27. __ Self-development is a major priority for him.
28. __ He finds feedback and criticism difficult to take.
29. __ People close to him say he is moody.
30. __ He often dismisses feelings or opinions that are different than his own.
31. __ He has no trouble standing up for what he believes.
32. __ He appreciates other people's honest feedback about himself.
33. __ He often magnifies problems.
34. __ He is looking for coaching and mentoring.
35. __ He is in the midst of a life change right now.
36. __ He asks a lot of those who love him.
37. __ He does not look for feedback from others. It is what he thinks that matters most.
38. __ He believes there are many ways to look at any situation.
39. __ He believes if he does not look out for himself, no one else will.
40. __ He tends to open up about himself and his past too early in a relationship.

SURVEY RESULTS

Compile your results as described below. This should take about ten minutes per survey.

1) Move the answers from the questions in the survey to the score sheet as indicated below.
2) Add up the scores in each column.
3) Write the sums in the appropriate quadrants in the box on page 207. Do the same with the sum totals for the surveys from family and friends.
4) Copy the scores to the similar box diagram on page 27.

SCORE SHEET:

	Self Score	Other #1	Other #2
#2	_____	_____	_____
#4	_____	_____	_____
#7	_____	_____	_____
#10	_____	_____	_____
#15	_____	_____	_____
#16	_____	_____	_____
#22	_____	_____	_____
#24	_____	_____	_____
#25	_____	_____	_____
#31	_____	_____	_____
SUM A =	_____	_____	_____

	Self Score	Other #1	Other #2
#1	_____	_____	_____
#9	_____	_____	_____
#18	_____	_____	_____
#20	_____	_____	_____
#21	_____	_____	_____
#27	_____	_____	_____
#32	_____	_____	_____
#34	_____	_____	_____
#35	_____	_____	_____
#38	_____	_____	_____
SUM B =	_____	_____	_____

	Self Score	Other #1	Other #2
#3	_____	_____	_____
#6	_____	_____	_____
#12	_____	_____	_____
#19	_____	_____	_____
#26	_____	_____	_____
#28	_____	_____	_____
#29	_____	_____	_____
#33	_____	_____	_____
#36	_____	_____	_____
#40	_____	_____	_____
SUM C =	_____	_____	_____

	Self Score	Other #1	Other #2
#5	_____	_____	_____
#8	_____	_____	_____
#11	_____	_____	_____
#13	_____	_____	_____
#14	_____	_____	_____
#17	_____	_____	_____
#23	_____	_____	_____
#30	_____	_____	_____
#37	_____	_____	_____
#39	_____	_____	_____
SUM D =	_____	_____	_____

Write the sums in the appropriate quadrants in the box on the facing page. Do the same with the sum totals for the surveys from family and friends. Then copy your scores to the similar box diagram on page 27.

The Emotional Zones

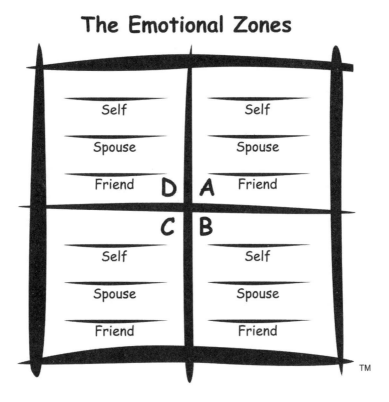

ENDNOTES

[1] *Halftime,* Bob Buford, Zondervan Publishing House p. 64.

[2] *Wild at Heart,* John Eldredge. Nashville: Thomas Nelson Publishers. p. 128.

[3] http://www.ccel.org/p/pascal/pensees/pensees.RTF, no. 139.

[4] This assessment is not offered as a definitive psychological test with well-developed statistical norms and standards. It was designed in consultation with human performance consultants and is a directional tool to aid in personal transformation.

ACKNOWLEDGEMENTS

I AM DEEPLY GRATEFUL FOR THE COMPANY OF THE FOLLOWING OUTSTANDING MEN:

My men's group—Michael Knowles, Tim Urquhart, Peter Hillen, Dave Scott, and Bruce Hawkins—for their support, encouragement, and willingness to learn and grow with me. Being with my band of brothers is like the days of old. King Arthur did not have better friends!

My accountability partners and lifelong friends Alex Somos and Chip Robinson: We have experienced more together than many could even dream. Thanks for reminding me of my vision and holding my feet to the fire.

Phil Geldart, you are a man of undying principle and have given generously of your time and resources to help me find my way. When I desperately needed a father, you were there. Your legacy is alive and well in the hearts of many men.

Bruce Etherington, you are my mentor, friend, encourager, and a networking superman.

Paul Henderson, you have led the way by taking off your armor and creating an immense chain reaction in other men. We salute you!

Fred Christmas, you have shown me how to stay young.

Bob Woodburne, when you say you love me, it still sounds fresh! I love you, too!

Rick Boersma, it has been a pleasure to work with you, my friend.

I HAVE BEEN BLESSED WITH A CARING AND DEVOTED FAMILY:

Cathy, words cannot express my love and gratitude to you for being my wife and constant companion. Without your prayer, perseverance, trust, support, and your undying love, only God knows where I would be today.

Alex, Benji, and Natalie, you are the most wonderful and amazing children, and my best friends. Stay real!

Mom and Dad, I honor you for staying together through the best and worst of times, learning and loving.

Angus and Ruth Henderson, you are the best in-laws, and you have never stopped praying for me—with good reason!

Uli and Carol Kortsch, no one has ever had a cooler uncle and aunt!

Leslie and Persis Bier, you are the ultimate grandparents. Your faith and life have been anchors in life's storms. I am looking forward to being with you again in eternity.

Members of the Vineyard family, you have modeled Jesus and his love for me.

I HAVE BEEN EXTREMELY FORTUNATE TO WORK WITH A TEAM OF EXCEPTIONAL PROFESSIONALS IN THE WRITING AND PRODUCTION OF THIS BOOK:

Deborah Gyapong, because of your coaching, writing expertise and editorial support, this book has captured everything I have wanted to say in a creative and accurate way. Thanks for your integrity, for keeping this project on the rails, and for pushing my writing hand.

Simon Presland, you are a solid brother who speaks with a similar heart and voice. Your edits and suggestions were masterful. Thank you for your commitment to going above and beyond the call of duty to see this project through.

Christy Petit, you caught the vision for this book early on and provided tremendous expertise for the *Look in the Mirror* surveys.

Haidee Ogden, you tirelessly translated digital notes and barely legible scribbles into a readable manuscript. It was wonderful working with you.

Tim Urquhart, you are a master at design. Thanks for your professional work on the cover and book illustrations.

Debbie Speers, thank you for creating a superb author photo.

Kevin Miller and his team at Fresh Wind Press, thank you for helping with the almost endless details in getting this project finalized, published, and marketed. You have been awesome.

WITHOUT THE FOLLOWING FRIENDS, THIS BOOK WOULD NOT HAVE BEEN WRITTEN:

My friends and colleagues at ISA (Instructional Systems Association) have been a wonderful part of my life. Heartfelt thanks to Ken Blanchard, Dean Anderson, Ron Galbraith, Dianne Hessan, and Stacey Murray. I am especially grateful to the late Terry Broomfield, whose passion and belief gave me a real kick in the pants.

Lynda Myler, you are a wonderful coach and encourager.

Chris Munford, thanks for the brutal workouts! You have shown me more of what is possible for this temporary body of mine.

To all my hardworking friends at Eagle's Flight: Thank you for providing the cash flow to help make this book possible.

Bobby John, you said you would not start your first book until I finished mine. It is time to pick up your pen!

FINALLY, I THANK JESUS CHRIST. YOU MAKE ALL THE DIFFERENCE, THROUGH YOUR SPIRIT IN ME. IT IS ALL FOR YOU.

ABOUT THE AUTHOR

D ave Loney is a performance coach, a dynamic presenter, an entrepreneur, and an innovator who enables individuals to reach their highest potential. His home base is EverGreen Ranch, a retreat center in Southern Ontario, where he facilitates workshops that create entrepreneurial, emotional, and spiritual breakthroughs. His programs and services enable executives and entrepreneurs to maximize their success, accelerate the realization of their life goals, and attain personal and professional life balance.

In 1988, Dave co-founded Eagle's Flight, a world leader in corporate experiential training, where he specialized in strategic development, international expansion, and new business ventures. He has trained leaders in many Fortune 500 companies. In 1996, he was recognized as a finalist for Ernst and Young's Entrepreneur of the Year Award.

Elected to the Board of Directors for the Instructional Systems Association, Dave was a panelist and presenter on many topics, including International Business Strategies, Innovative Marketing, and Managing Exponential Growth.

Dave also leads a men's group, which meets weekly for mutual encouragement, accountability, and personal and spiritual growth.

To contact Dave or to obtain information about coaching programs offered at Evergreen Ranch, speeches, seminars, and Sweating From Your Eyes workshops, please visit www.EverGreenRanch.ca. E-mail: dave@sweatingfromyoureyes.com. Write: EverGreen Ranch R.R. #3 Rockwood, Ontario, Canada N0B 2K0. Call toll free: 1-888-335-5864. Local: (519) 767-6606. To find a men's group in your area, please go to the links page at www.sweatingfromyoureyes.com.